REVIEWS FOR

Ultra Productive

Matthew is proof that it's never too late [or too early] to turn your life around. The person you were yesterday doesn't have to be the person you'll be tomorrow. Reading books changed my life for the better and it did the same for Matthew. Through the power of reading, and other self-improvement activities, Matthew was able to believe in himself and ultimately live a richer and fuller life.

—**Alex Wieckowski** – Podcaster, Author of *The Readers Journey* and Founder of *Alex & Books.*

.

***

Matt Worthington walks the walk he describes in his book. His journey to becoming a productive citizen speaks to one of his basic pieces of advice: surround yourself with people who you admire and who do things you want to do, and you'll be better for it. Matt has come a long way, and with this book, I hope he can invite others to walk the walk, too.

– **Carl Shepherd** - Cofounder and Former Chief Strategy Officer of *HomeAway Inc.*

***

Matt takes "self-help" to another level. His own journey of overcoming adversity and his determination to make a better life for himself is deeply inspiring. Matt's methods clearly helped him through his own struggles, but more widely, they will prove to help so many others.

– **Patrick Lyons** – TEDx Speaker, YouTuber and CEO of *The Lyon Shred.*

i

***

Worthington's book is a riveting story that gets all the emotions of the reader involved. The lessons he teaches are universal, and if followed, can help the reader overcome even the toughest obstacles in life. Worthington uses his story in a way that can relate to all. His process of overcoming adversity to make a better life is evident and compelling.

– **Kacy Benson** – Speaker, Comedian and Author of *The Crash: Overcoming When Life Falls Apart.*

***

Matt's story is an inspirational message about the power of HOPE through encouragement and compassion. His transformative personal journey can give HOPE to community college students across the country. As Chancellor of Austin Community College, I am proud to know Matt as a distinguished member of the ACC Riverbat family.

– **Dr. Richard Rhodes** – President of *Austin Community College.*

Ultra Productive:

Graduating Debt-Free & Getting Ahead

MATT WORTHINGTON

Published by KHARIS PUBLISHING, imprint of KHARIS MEDIA LLC.

ISBN-13: 978-1-946277-83-1
ISBN-10: 1-946277-83-5

Library of Congress Control Number: 2020951553

All KHARIS PUBLISHING products are available at special quantity discounts for bulk purchase for sales promotions, premiums, fund-raising, and educational needs. For details, contact:

Kharis Media LLC
Tel: 1-479-599-8657
support@kharispublishing.com
www.kharispublishing.com

Do you want more out of life than this?

You're a winner. That's right—you're a winner. You know why? Because you are here. You're a winner because you're reading this; because you care about getting ahead; because you are brave enough to take on the challenge's college brings. You're a winner because you know you can make a difference in this world, and for this reason, I promise you will.

If you follow the ideas in this book, you will have more money, less stress, and a greater sense of purpose. You will be hungrier for success, more disciplined, and more driven than ever before.

By changing bad habits little by little, establishing new routines that encourage growth, and by challenging yourself every day, your life will begin to change in ways you never thought possible. It all starts right now.

Are you ready for this journey? Are you ready for your life to change? Are you ready to graduate college debt-free? Do you believe that you can do it? Guess there's only one way to find out.

"Great art comes from the depth of one's being". - Unknown

DISCLAIMER

If you are a woman, I do not want you to perceive this reading for all its 'he's' and 'man's' as discrimination, or the leaving out of the feminine. This book is not intended to be interpreted that way. If you are reading this and it resonates with you, it doesn't matter what gender or sex you are blessed with. This text carries a truth that transcends gender and I trust that you will not perceive the manner in which it was written as a negative. I did think about changing the words when I was writing them, incorporating he and she. However, I refrained from doing so, as I felt it would change the text to a degree in which it was not intended. Therefore, I am including this disclaimer at the outset.

I understand that not everyone grew up the same way I did. I understand that it is highly probable that our backgrounds are vastly different. I am also conscious of the fact that the position my parents put me in, and the color of my skin, have made my path to financial freedom less challenging. Further, I tried to acknowledge that the city I grew up in gave me access to highly successful mentors who took me under their wing. I tried my best to take this into account and recognize that my audience may have differences in financial and familial situations to a degree in which I may never understand.

Next, I must mention that this book is based on a traditional four-year, undergraduate program rather than the academic timeline that may include graduate school, law school, or medical school. I must also mention the age demographic I intend to influence is targeted between fourteen and twenty-four. I believe this age demographic will benefit the most from this book—despite its relevance on a universal level.

These lessons can still help you graduate debt-free no matter your age or circumstance; but, readers between the ages of fourteen and twenty-four will benefit the most because the stories and experiences I share take place during these same years of my life. Therefore, my advice and insight follow a narrow timeline of events.

I must also mention that this book is not an alternate formula on how to refinance your student debt. If you want to do this, look into companies such as SoFi, Avant, and LendingTree. Rather, this is my autobiography. I am not an expert on this topic, nor have I done any additional research. I'm just sharing my story as I experienced it. This is not a 'one size fits all' book. It's mere guidance for a hopeful conclusion of similar results.

This book highlights how I was able to graduate debt-free. These things worked best for me but I can't promise they will work the same for you. However, I personally believe that if studied properly and mimicked closely, most of the core values, lessons, and stories that I share and experienced can be used for anyone and everyone that is trying to graduate college debt-free.

With that said, I still encourage you to find what works best for you. This book does not cover it all—so get creative. Let my story inspire you and help you start on the right foot. Ultimately, it is your own effort, belief, discipline, and hunger that will determine your success following the completion of this book.

Lastly, I must mention that the redundancies in this book serve a purpose. The more you read something, then read it over again, the higher chance you'll remember it. Draw from this book the bits and pieces that remind you of why you started on this journey. Then continue to look at the quotes, one liners, and phrases to keep you accountable and motivated in achieving your goals.

WHY I WROTE THIS BOOK

I wrote this book because I want to help those of you who are willing to try to get one step ahead. It wasn't easy for me and I promise it won't be easy for you. But it changed my life and I strongly believe my story and the lessons I learned will change yours too.

It was all worth it in the end. I hope you all enjoy hearing about this path as much as I enjoy looking back on it.

At the minimum, I hope this book can serve as a form of entertainment for all of you. If you don't graduate college debt-free, my hope is that you would at least have enjoyed the story and the lessons. There really is beauty in the struggle.

The last thing I must mention is, I realize that I'm nothing special. I am no more interesting than any of you. I told myself I would not turn this instruction manual for college debt into a memoir. However, without me including my upbringing, it would be hard for you to understand how my adolescence shaped my adult years.

The environment in which I was raised, and my family life, are a part of my early troubles but also my latter successes. The shortcomings that I created for myself in my head proved near fatal, but my moment of enlightenment made me realize how beautiful my early life truly was, how incredible my parents truly were, and how I was able to break free from the limitations I placed on myself.

This story will take a dive inside my mind. My transparency will leave no stone unturned and my openness will allow you to make sense of it all. My hope is that you can relate to the good and the bad, then make better decisions then I did. Excited to hear of your successes!

Yours truly,

Matt Worthington

OPENING MESSAGE

Life is tough. It is really, really tough. But there is always a way out. And I'm here to help in the process of that.

I'm a strong believer that if you follow in my footsteps, you will see drastic changes in your life. You will slowly get closer to becoming the best version of yourself, grow as a person and reach your fullest potential. A little hard work goes a long way; just a little effort and you will start seeing enormous differences in your day-to-day life.

If you're not trying to become a better person today than you were yesterday, you're missing out on the best part of life. Everybody is living but not everybody lives. You only live when you try to become a better version of yourself every day. You can't go back in time and fix mistakes that you've made, but you can learn from those mistakes and use them to grow.

Take a step back and be a critic of your own life. Is the person you are right now the person that you want to be? The answer should be no. The person you should want to be is you in ten years. Always chase a better version of yourself.

We all have room to improve; nobody is perfect. But there are things that you can change right now. Are you investing the proper time and energy into yourself? Are you fully satisfied with your life up to this point? Have you accomplished every goal you've ever set for yourself? Probably not. But that's okay.

This book will help you learn how to put more energy into the things you care about. At the top of that list should be your own personal growth: mentally, physically, and emotionally. You can completely alter your life path, completely change the person you are, and take the first step toward becoming the person you always wanted to be. Your time is now!

Acknowledgements

This book started as a big, messy thing and required more than just my own brain power to make something legible out of it.

First and foremost, I am indebted to the amazing staff at Kharis Publishing, especially Francis E. Umesiri, PHD., who gave me the opportunity to write this book. Without you, none of this would have been possible. Not only has your story inspired me, but your constant feedback during the writing process was indispensable.

To my family, for putting up with my sh*t all these years and continuing to love me anyway. You are my sources of daily inspiration. Without your love and support, this journey would have never started. Thank you for believing in me and encouraging my every move. You gave me a fighting chance in this difficult world, and I'll be forever grateful for that.

To my friends and mentors, thank you for seeing in me what I couldn't see in myself. You helped me grasp the idea that I could truly make a difference in this world. Without your support, I would have never found my light. Thank you for acknowledging my crazy ideas, for your patience during my darker years, and for your unconditional love. I never sensed an ounce of doubt, and for that, I thank you.

To Greg Sears, if you are out there, I hope this catches you. When I was down and out, you were there to show me the way. You taught me to accept myself for who I was, you introduced the concepts of Think & Grow Rich, and you reminded me that it's not about the size of the dog in the fight, but the size of the fight in the dog. I owe my successes to you.

To Bruce Howard, it was the meeting I had with you that helped me graduate debt-free. You had faith in my abilities, faith in my plan and without your reassurance, I would have taken a completely different route. You were the difference maker during my last semester of college.

To Cody Woolley, it was the car ride from Austin to San Antonio that changed my life. Your advice has helped me stay sober all these years. Thank you for your constant love and support, brother. You have touched many lives, I'm lucky that one of them was mine.

There is nothing that brings me more joy and happiness in this world than waking up every day and having the opportunity to help others. My life wouldn't be what it is today if I weren't surrounded by so many amazing people. To the rest of you who have believed in me and helped me over the years, I thank you. As it would be too difficult for me to list all of you, I would like to acknowledge your support.

Thank you for helping me find my way, so that I could help others do the same.

CHAPTER 1

HOW WE GOT HERE

In the eyes of many, higher education has become a necessary component to the successful futures of young Americans. The need for a college degree is more pertinent now, than any other time in history. We hear over and over that in order to get hired at a respectable company, in order to make a good living, and in order to be respected amongst your peers, you need to go to college. I don't completely agree with this, but fear gets in the way.

Fear of failure. Fear of financial destitution. Fear of peer perception.

I get this. I was there too. Unfortunately, this probably won't change. So, let's just accept that you're going to go or you're already in college. This is totally fine, I'm all for education and learning. However, there is one BIG problem: it's outrageously expensive. University tuition prices have skyrocketed nationwide.

This spike in tuition pricing has left hard working parents searching for additional ways to put their kids through college, while still trying to make ends meet. For the middle to lower class, the constant increase in tuition pricing has left these families financially shell shocked.

To add fuel to the fire, Human Resource departments turn down applicants all together if they see no form of higher education listed on their resumes. This has made it increasingly hard for non-college goers to land decent paying jobs and has left parents either unable or unwilling to take on this financial burden themselves.

This has left young adults with a very important decision and a very difficult trade-off: Get a college-level education and end up with potentially huge amounts of debt so you can get a decent paying job upon graduation or save the time and money on college but accept a job that may start only a few bucks an hour above minimum wage or thousands of dollars less a year compared to the salary of a college graduate.

What has this created? The college debt epidemic.

THE COLLEGE DEBT EPIDEMIC

Let's look at some facts.[1]

- The national total of combined student debt is now over $1.5 trillion.

- College tuition prices have more than doubled since the 1980s.

- More than 3 million senior citizens in the US are still paying off their student loans.

- As many as 40% of borrowers could default on their student loans by 2023.

- Of people who use a bankruptcy-assistance service to file for Chapter 7 bankruptcy protection, 32% carry student-loan debt.

- Student-loan debt is the reason 13% of Americans in a survey conducted last year said they decided not to have kids.

- Nearly 50% of millennials who have or had student-loan debt think college wasn't worthwhile.

RIDICULOUSNESS

In the 90s, the government stopped regulating tuition costs and allowed universities to set their own prices on tuition. Some universities now cost double, triple, or even quadruple of what the cost of tuition was in previous decades. And no, this is NOT due to inflation alone. There is much more to this story.

College became a business.

Going to college was once something that almost everyone could do. Now, it's almost a luxury because not everyone can afford the outrageous tuition prices. By going to college, you are draining either your parents' life savings or your own, so that you can get an education to land a job that will support you enough to allow your future kids the opportunity to go to college themselves. Then, when your kids go to college, you're potentially having your life

---

[1] https://www.businessinsider.com/student-loan-debt-crisis-college-cost-mind-blowing-facts-2019-7#11-nearly-50-of-millennials-who-have-or-had-student-loan-debt-think-college-wasnt-worthwhile-11

savings drained all over again so that your kids don't have the same burden weighing on them.

If you aren't lucky enough to have the financial means to pay for your kid's college tuition, then the cycle of loans and student debt continues with your offspring. Until someone breaks this generational barrier, our lives are consumed in college tuition and the American education system. Here's a likely scenario for today's student:

a)   12 years of our adolescence in school to prepare for college

b)   4-12 years in college

c)   10-20 years paying off our student loans

d)   10-20 years saving for your kids' college funds

e)   5-10 years helping your kids' pay off their own college debt

Having this much of our lives consumed in education—and the expenses that come along with it—doesn't feel right. But this price fixing is the reality we live in, and the college debt epidemic will only get worse—unless someone can change the way we look at it…

DON'T LISTEN TO SOCIETY

The college debt epidemic is real. At the same time, this term, "the college debt epidemic", is societal propaganda. It creates a false sense of communal togetherness. Not everyone has to graduate college with debt. Not everyone should think graduating college with debt is normal. Students should not submit to these norms.

But that is not the case. Society has made college debt a normal thing.

"It's just part of life."

"Everyone takes out student loans."

But I refuse to believe this. I refuse to believe that it's normal to have to pay off your student loans for 18.5 years. *Yes, 18.5 years.* This is the national average according to Forbes.

Why should we accept that over a fourth of our lives should be spent trying to pay off school? A fourth of our lives—on top of what we already spent in school and another fourth of our life that we will spend putting our children through college. If you choose to have kids, putting enough money aside for a college fund can easily take fifteen to twenty years. This means, three-fourths of our lives are tied into the American education system. Now this just doesn't seem right to me. I can't be the only one who feels this way.

I think what needs to change is our mindset. The knowingness that this can be fixed. Maybe not from a governmental standpoint, but from within our-selves. With a little more planning during high school, with harder work dur-ing college, and a burning desire not to fall into societal norms, college debt can become your battle to win. This "epidemic" won't change until you change the way you view it. It takes hard work. It takes grit. It takes consistent action. But at least it won't add stress to your life after you graduate.

I'll say this now and again throughout this book. You don't have to fall into this stereotype. You don't need to graduate with college debt. This is blas-phemy. Work your butt off starting right now and graduate college debt-free.

If you want to break these norms, then listen closely. I'm here to give you my secret formula. The formula that will knock those numbers down fifteen to twenty years. But first, let me take you to where it all started: my childhood.

The following five chapters, will focus on my story—my personal life and the events that led up to my transformation. To continue learning about the concepts of graduating college debt-free, skip ahead to Chapter 7.

CHAPTER 2

MY STORY

I came from modest beginnings. Blessed, but humble. A family of six—two sisters, one brother, and happily married parents. My mom was an immigrant from Europe and my dad, the youngest of five from a small farming town in Iowa. My parents were both extremely hard working and did all they could to make sure we had the best life possible. However, my family situation was different from most; my dad was paralyzed.

On a late drunken night in his twenties, my dad was riding in the passenger seat without a seatbelt. His fraternity brother, who claimed to be sober, was driving them back from a party when disaster struck. At about one o'clock in the morning, my dad's fraternity brother fell asleep at the wheel and the car veered off the side of the road.

Going nearly 60 miles per hour, they hit a utility pole.

My dad flew through the front windshield, slamming his head and neck up through the glass. The impact severed his spine, leaving him paralyzed from the neck down. By the grace of God, my dad slowly got movement back in his upper body but has not been able to walk since.

After meeting my mom overseas, getting married and starting a family, my dad began working for a non-profit organization. During the earlier years of his career, he was able to work. However, as time went on, it was too much for his body to handle. The long hours sitting in his wheelchair at work gave him sores and constant pain. He had to step away, leaving my mom in charge of making the money.

With four kids and only one main source of income, money was tight. My parents did all they could to save and continue to provide us with all the things a kid could dream of. It was enough, more than enough, but I was plagued with an inferiority complex.

The fact that my dad was paralyzed messed with my head. My dad could do just about everything a classic able-bodied dad could do: go hunting and fishing, pass the football, take us camping, work on cars, and grill burgers. But it always felt different. I always felt like the ugly duckling when other kids would stare. I wasn't sure how other kids thought of it, how other kids thought of me. I always felt less than, felt as if I had gotten the short end of the stick.

5

During my adolescent years, I couldn't shake this feeling of being different. I felt disadvantaged. This hurt. And as a kid, I couldn't see the big picture. I couldn't see all that I was blessed with or even the positives that came with having a dad that was paralyzed. Instead, I was stuck on being different. This thought was overpowering, and it began to consume me.

Years went by, and I got older. But I could never shake this thought. It led me to being extremely lonely. Deep down I was hurting. I felt like I couldn't relate to anyone, like others didn't understand. I also felt like I had been wronged.

Then, things got extra tough when my dad got sick.

SICKNESS

Throughout my entire childhood, my dad was in and out of the hospital. Aside from the dozens of surgeries, he managed decently well. He was completely independent and didn't need nurses to come by the house to assist him in his day-to-day routine. My dad was much stronger than that.

He hated help, and just about refused it. He hated feeling like a burden to others, so he wasn't. He didn't use his situation as an excuse to get extra help, extra attention or extra pity. He did things his own way and he made it work.

He managed to take care of the house, run the errands, file the taxes, pay the bills. He cooked dinner for us nearly every night for eighteen years. He was a gentle, supportive, charismatic, and loving man. He didn't whine or complain. He just did what he had to do, and he did a damn good job.

As time went on, my dad began to get increasingly frail. He began to lose weight and lose mobility in his arms and shoulders.

During my junior year of college, my dad's health took a turn for the worse. His weak core and failing spine disagreed with his already progressing scoliosis. He leaned so far to the right that his lower rib and upper hip bones began to grind against each other. Pieces of bone, tissue, and muscle broke off which led to a pocket of fluid that built up in his side. A massive abscess the size of a basketball developed.

Doctors figured it was a simple fix. Remove the abscess, insert a 'vac' for a few weeks to remove the excess drainage, sew him back up, and he would be good to go. The surgery took place, and all was well. But the fluid never stopped coming. And the 'vac' continued to fill completely.

Doctors where confused. They didn't know where the fluid kept coming from. They listed the case as a medical mystery, but told my dad he'd be fine.

The result of the surgeries and the removal of the abscess left a massive cavity on the side of his stomach. In order to clean the wound and limit the amount of fluid that seeped out, nurses would stick their entire hands up inside my dad's side and stuff it with dozens of pieces of gauze. The exposure to the air and improper cleaning of the wound resulted in ongoing infections.

Over and over my dad had to fight past the fevers and the cold sweats. He had to fight through the emergency room visits and going septic. He had to fight through the emergency surgeries and the washouts. He had to fight through the constant pain and nausea. The dehydration, the malnutrition, the wandering mind of being in an isolated hospital room week after week.

My dad fought. And he fought hard. But there is only so much one can handle. He went back into the hospital and told the staff he wanted to be listed as DNR, Do not resuscitate. His life was is the hands of the Lord.

Mentally, physically and spiritually he was exhausted. His quality of life worsened and he needed to catch a break. But a break never came.

My dad went from 155 pounds to 125 pounds in a matter of two months. At six foot, five inches, you can imagine how frail he looked.

He began to have trouble eating meals and getting himself out of bed. He slept longer than he was awake during the day. He started having erratic behavior and forgetting things often. He would try and stay home so he could be around our family but would get so sick after a few days that he would have to go back into the hospital.

Things continued to get worse. It would take him fifteen minutes just to put on his shoes and twice as long to clean himself up in the mornings. I remember him being so sick one day that he could barely open the door to his car. His hand was shaking so badly that he couldn't fit the key in the slot. He had chills throughout the day and no matter how warm it got inside; he couldn't stop shivering.

Despite being cold, my dad would sweat nonstop. He used to lay out towels in our backyard that he had used to dry himself off. There were times when our entire clothing line in the backyard was fully lined up with his sweaty towels. It was awful seeing that. It was awful seeing him get weaker. It was awful watching my dad die right in front of my eyes.

He wanted so badly to make it to see all us kids live the life he had worked so hard to give to us. But he was in pain. Constant pain. Pain that keeps you up at night. And the sweats and chills made life unbearable for him. He continued to get weaker and weaker.

Hospice began to call the house. And this is when I knew his time was close.

My dad had no strength but fought for us anyway. He lived by the quote: "The real hero is the man who fights even though he is scared."

He didn't know if he'd wake up after falling asleep. He said his Hail Mary's every night before he closed his eyes just in case God took him during the calmness of the night. He didn't know when his last breath would be, and it was tough. Not only on him, but on all of us.

WHEN IT RAINS IT POURS

On a fall morning later that year, I woke up suddenly with a weird feeling in my stomach. I got out of the bed, left the room, and uneasily walked about my house. I could hear my dad in his room making some noise which was weird because he usually slept in on Saturday mornings.

Every step towards my dad's room was another step closer to an unsettling reality. My dad was in the room packing his bags, which usually meant he wasn't feeling well and was headed back into the Emergency Room. This was normal. However, this time it felt different.

There was an uneasy atmosphere in the room. I asked my dad if everything was okay and he paused what he was doing, put down his bags and tried to find the strength to talk. He was having trouble getting out what he wanted to say, but I patiently waited because I knew whatever it was, it was going to be important. With trembling lips and watery eyes, my dad looked directly at me and said six words I will never forget:

"I've lost the will to fight."

There was a long pause between us. I don't think the severity of the situation had hit me up until that point. He told me he was exhausted—physically, emotionally, and spiritually. He was ready for the good Lord to take him home. He had lost the will to fight. Lost the will to live.

My dad went back into the hospital and put his life in the hands of the Lord. He was given medications, got hooked up to IV's, had his nutritional intake monitored and had help packing and repacking the fluid vacuum that was inserted into his stomach.

I did my best to visit him as much as I could. However, it was tough for me because I was never open with others about what was going on with my dad. I always kept things behind closed doors. All my friends would share their location with each other on their phones, but I didn't because I didn't want anybody to know I was always at the hospital with my dad. I didn't want my problems to be anybody else's problem. I didn't want my burden to weigh on those around me, so I just kept to myself and was constantly secretive as to where I was.

During this time, it was hard for me to stay positive—especially when my mom got injured. On top of all that was going on with my dad, my mom had an awful accident in our backyard that nearly killed her. She was working out in the yard when a tree fell only inches from the top of her head, nearly crushing her skull. Luckily, she managed to survive. Her ER visit resulted in twenty-eight staples in her head, a fractured vertebra, a severe concussion, and a deep skin abrasion.

I felt like I couldn't catch a break. I wanted so badly to share with others the emotional pain I was feeling. I wanted to share with others that I felt like giving up, but I stopped myself from doing so because I felt like there was always more I could be doing, and always others expecting something from me.

I felt like when I was going out to see friends, I should have really been at home helping my mom with chores. When I was out partying, I felt like I should be visiting my dad in the hospital. Yet, when I was in the hospital or helping my mom and siblings, I felt as if I was missing out on everything that other kids my age were doing. I was in this terrible middle spot, never doing 100 percent of what I wanted to do.

I felt like my family relied on me, but I was losing friends because I couldn't commit my time and energy to them. It was an endless cycle, but I couldn't break away from it because I felt like I had a lot of people counting on me.

Looking back, I chose to put my life on pause because I didn't want to have any regrets if my dad were to pass. I didn't want to regret not seeing him enough or regret not spending enough time with him while he was still around. So, I made it my goal to spend as much time with him as I could, and that's what I did.

I spent every second I could with my dad while he was in the hospital. The

National championship, the Super Bowl, two seasons of March madness. A full season of college football. Birthdays at the hospital. Father's Day at the hospital. Graduation at the hospital. First day on the job at the hospital. National intern of the year at the hospital. Valentine's Day at the hospital. Easter at the hospital. Mother's Day at the hospital.

That hospital room was a second home to me just as much as it had become for my dad. For my mom too. She continued to stay the night at the hospital with my dad for days at a time. Missing work and not coming home so she come be there for him. She and I had the hospital address saved in our phones because we were there so often. And every time we thought things were going to get better, they'd just get worse. Another surgery, another operation, another procedure.

There was a part of me that wanted to believe that my dad was getting better but every time something else would happen. He began sleeping longer, getting out of his bed less and eating next to nothing. Home health and nurses came by daily to help clean his wounds and help him with his daily activities.

I realized he was never going to get better. It was the beginning of the end. The doctors were just doing what they could to give him a few more weeks, time after time again. It was a heavy burden to carry.

We could see the end of my dad's life on the horizon.

I knew at some point I would need to truly become the man of the house because my dad wouldn't be around. This was a tough time in my life but one that I used to build character. As difficult as it was, I did my best to use it as a chance to better the man I was. I strived to be a harder worker, a better son, a better brother. A stronger man mentally, physically, and spiritually. I used this time to test my strength.

I didn't let the situation with my dad slow me down. Instead, I began to use it as a motivation to work harder. I felt like my name was called on and I needed to be the one to step up to the plate. I felt like I had a chip on my shoulder. I felt like I had something to prove—to make my dad proud. I had to do things not because I wanted to, but because I had no other choice. I had to be the one to take care of my family.

Everyone has a story, and everyone has troubles. Nobody's family situation is perfect. The odds will always be stacked against you and the path to success will always be a difficult one. But you just do what you gotta do.

Instead of making the situation you're in worse than it already is, do something about it. Be the change in your life that you've been looking for. You are the superhero that you keep envisioning in your mind to come save the day. You hold deep within you the magic remedy that will wipe out all the pain and sorrow.

Change your mindset, change your perspective, and you'll change your life. You will fail and succeed every day, but by not letting your situation control you, you will fall in love with the process and see the beauty in all the darkness you face.

"Character is only revealed in a crisis, not defined. Don't let your circumstance determine your outcome." – Paul TP Wong

CHAPTER 3

WHITE LIGHT

There is no denying that my dad's health was a rollercoaster during college. He would be in the hospital for weeks and sometimes even months at a time; big surgeries, small surgeries, big operations, small operations. Week in, week out. It went on and on. Always the same story.

In between one of these operations, my dad was recovering and was expected to come home soon. Unexpectedly, the sutures from an earlier surgery came undone. An artery burst, and blood started spewing rapidly all over the hospital room. Neither the nurse nor my dad was able to apply pressure firm enough to stop the bleeding. My dad started to lose blood quickly.

The nurses rushed him into emergency surgery. His chances of surviving were slim. The nurses didn't think he'd make it. He had already lost so much blood that it was unlikely he would wake. After hours on the operating table my dad made it. But he wasn't looking to good.

I went to the ICU to see my dad that night. Seeing him in the ICU with a breathing tube broke my heart. He knew my sister and I were there, but he couldn't talk. All you could see were tears building up in his eyes as he looked at us helplessly.

Tears fell down his cheeks as he was fighting for his life.

There was nothing he could do. He was so weak he could barely keep his eyes open. He couldn't talk so there was no way of expressing how he felt. He was stuck.

His strength came and went throughout the night as his physical form took precedence over his spiritual mind. At one point he would be strong and express we had nothing to worry about because he wasn't going anywhere; the next, he would write on a white board the nurses gave him and say it was close to the end. This went on for a few hours until he had no more strength to give. His eyes closed, and we walked out of that hospital room not knowing if he'd ever wake back up.

GOD IS REAL

Days later, my dad returned home. He was encouragingly optimistic, warm, and content. I couldn't help but wonder why the change in spirit? He told me the most beautiful story I had ever heard. This is how it went:

My dad's account during his emergency surgery on October 28th, 2019:

Jeff Worthington:

It was just like any other night. I had just finished watching some TV and the nurse came in to help me get situated for bed. As she was putting fresh sheets on my bed, she noticed that I didn't look too good. She said, "Jeff, how are you feeling? Your face looks flushed."

I too, then started to notice that I didn't feel 100 percent. Now that she pointed it out, I felt quite bad. She pulled back some of the covers to look at my wound and gasped.

As she peeled back the bandage, blood started going everywhere. It looked like a broken fire hydrant. One of my sutures had come undone and blood was spilling out. Fast.

She grabbed her radio and called for immediate back up, then she jumped onto my bed and straddled me so she could apply the necessary amount of pressure to my now opened wound. Other nurses rushed into the room. The nurse that was still with me was doing her best to apply pressure to keep me from bleeding out. Our eyes locked and I'll never forget the look she gave me as she barked out orders to the rest of her team.

She was trying to make sure I didn't die before I got to the operating table.

I was losing so much blood that I began coming in and out of consciousness. I started to see stars. My vision got darker and darker and the last thing I remember was not being able to see anything. All I could hear were the surgeons preparing to cut me open. I whispered, "DNR, DNR."

The surgeon said, "What the hell is DNR?!"

There was a slight pause "…Do Not Resuscitate," the nurse responded, "If he flatlines, there's no coming back," she continued. They threw me up on the operating table then…

Am I dead? Why am I still awake?

I was outside of my body looking down over myself. There were a dozen people in the room around me. Surgeons calling out for instruments, techs and nurses responding. Health care workers coming in and out of the room. Monitors beeping and surgical displays ringing. Vitals being checked and teams supervised. People in scrubs were working all around me and they were moving fast.

As I continued to watch I couldn't help but notice how peaceful I felt. There was a beautiful white light to my back and a stillness in the air. The light to my back was unlike anything I had ever seen before. It was so beautiful that it's hard to describe how it looked. I've never felt so calm and content in my entire life.

Coming from the white light was my dad reaching out to me. He was sitting poolside, in a speedo, grinning from cheek to cheek. He continued to reach out and tell me it was okay if I wanted to come home. I was ready. It was time to be at peace. No pain, no sorrow, no anxiety, no fear.

I began to reach out. The closer I got, the happier I became. I was ready to come home. But as our hands began to touch, my eyes opened and starting down at me was the surgeon I had heard talking right before I blacked out.

REFLECTION

The white board from that night in the ICU.

The white light my dad saw were the gates of heaven, the kingdom of the Lord. Angels were opening the gates for my dad to come home so that he could feel eternal peace in the resting place for the righteous. He was getting his wings but it was not his time.

And a poem I wrote based on the story that he told me:

POEM – WHITE LIGHT

Lord, give me my wings

White light, the resting place for the righteous

White light, home of the finest

White light, calmness, peace and quiet

White light, the kingdom of God, you can't hide it

White light, where the memories are timeless

White light, tranquility compliments the brightness

White light, warmth, and peace in the house of the highest

We will meet again, white light, when you're ready to take me home

Face to face with big laughs and tight speedos

Your hand reaching out, almost touching…so close

A moment in time, I wish I could have froze

But here I am, in this fight, I'll know when I know

Until then, white light, I'll prepare for your throne

BITTERNESS

I was bitter at the fact my parents couldn't send me off to a four-year university like all my other friends. After my first year at community college, I quickly realized this was a silver lining. As my dad's health declined, our relationship heightened.

When I was away from the hospital, I used to take pictures of everything I did so I could document my life and share those memories with my dad since he was too sick to experience the special moments with me. I knew he wouldn't be around for much longer, so I wanted to share as many moments with him as possible to make up for the inevitable lost time.

Despite him not physically being there with me on all my trips, he would be able to share the memories with me through my pictures and videos that I'd bring home to him.

My dad spent hours every day looking at the same IV's and the same hospital walls every day. He talked to the same nurses and the same doctors. He ate the same food and had the same protein shakes. He couldn't get out and continue living life. So, I'd document these special moments to give him a piece of freedom from his own mind.

People and moments pass quickly. If you have the chance to capture a special moment, do it. Nothing made my dad happier than continuing to live life with us through the lens of our cameras.

Our relationship continued to grow as he watched us achieve and experience the beauty the world has to offer. We continued to do what we loved, live out our dreams and follow our passions and he was there to see it. Being able to share these important times together, despite his health declining, was something I'll never forget.

"Feeling grateful or appreciative of something in your life actually attracts more of the things that you appreciate and value into your life." – Northrup Christiane

CHAPTER 4

SUBSTANCES CAN RUIN

Breaking away from the chains of alcohol was the greatest thing to ever happen to me. However, it was not easy. I was an alcoholic for four years. Four years before I even turned eighteen. I depended on alcohol to do homework. I depended on alcohol to go out and socialize. I depended on alcohol when I was sad, upset, scared, or stressed.

Alcohol was my crutch for anything and everything that was hard in my life. I didn't have the mental toughness and disciple to hold myself upright when things were difficult. Alcohol always made everything better.

When my dad got sick in college, I wanted to run to the bottle, but I knew I couldn't. Naturally, the harder things got, the more I wanted to drink. However, the more I would drink, the more I would hurt. Just years before, I experienced this firsthand.

At the ripe age of eighteen, things in my life fell apart. My life was in shambles. I was mentally, physically, and financially drained. I hit rock bottom and can honestly say, alcohol brought me to my knees.

HIGH SCHOOL

Of all my friends, my future after graduating high school was probably the most questionable. The things I did in high school—the person I was—and my view on life created a sense of uncertainty when discussing what was next for me. However, I knew that I wanted to be someone. I wanted to make a difference and be remembered, for the good, not the bad.

My failures in sports during high school made me hungry to prove myself in other ways. If I couldn't be the best in athletics, then I told myself I would be the best with girls, most liked by peers, and make the most money. It worked. I got a lot of attention. More than what was good for me. Attention not for how intelligent I was or how hard I worked, but instead for how wild I was, how much I partied, and how many girls I slept with.

I would go to class drunk, talk back to my teachers, and show up late. I was disruptive and disrespectful. I cheated on tests, partied on the weekends, and took nothing seriously.

17

I was always on my high horse and thought the spotlight was always on me. I felt like I ran the show and I told myself I was the coolest kid at the entire school. I let the girls and the partying get to my head. I was narcissistic, selfish, reckless, and inconsiderate. I was too shallow to realize that in the real world all that didn't matter.

Like most of us, I just wanted to fit in.

Once I graduated high school, I completely dismantled the persona that I had created for myself over those four years. I knew the reputation I had and the person everyone thought me to be, and I hated it. But it was hard for me to adjust from being on top of the world, getting practically anyone and anything, to being a nobody in my eyes. I knew it would take some time to get over myself, break free from my egotism, and find my purpose. Unfortunately, I quickly fell back on old habits and this is when things got worse.

I continued to try and live in that past but found myself to be filled with guilt, shame and discontent. I couldn't stand myself. I was disgusted and ashamed with who I was becoming and didn't want to live anymore. I began to drink heavily to ease the pain and my life became unmanageable.

ALCOHOL WAS MY COPING MECHANISM

I had a love-hate relationship with alcohol. I loved that it helped me forget the troubles of the day, but I hated that I relied on it to do so. I loved that it numbed my pain, but I hated that I was hurting. I loved that it made me confident in my own skin but hated that I wasn't without it. Ultimately, it was a battle.

And my battle with alcohol led me to the darkest places I had ever been.

We all wear masks. We put on a front to make sure others don't see our hurt, our pain and our struggles. I may have looked happy, confident, and secure, but deep down there was a lot going on. I was constantly hurting. This led me to look for something to ease the pain. Alcohol gave me this comfort.

Alcohol allowed me to escape my own mind. It allowed me to escape my thoughts. I loved it so much that it became all that I did. Drinking consumed me just as much as I consumed it. I kept chasing that feeling everywhere I went, with everything I did, but nothing quite did the trick like a drink did.

Alcohol had been so good to me. I loved it so much that I couldn't control my drinking. I could never get enough. It took over my life, then played tricks on my mind worse than anything I had been dealing with prior. Alcohol re-wired the chemical balance in my brain and instead of producing a high like it once did, it produced an imbalance that drove me to suicide. When you fly too high, you're destined to fall—and I got a little too close to the sun.

CHAPTER 5

NOVEMBER 14™ 2016

HOPELESS, DESPERATE, VULNERABLE

No matter how good of a front other people put on, there are always things going on behind closed doors that others don't see. Everyone tries to mask their pain and suffering. A lot of people are dying on the inside. Sadly, we see more fake smiles then we realize.

It is the people whose lives seem perfect that are actually going through it the most. In this day and age, it's considered weak to be open with others about your issues. Instead, everyone acts as if their lives are perfectly fine. We choose to keep what's bothering us bottled up on the inside. But by not talking about your problems, you create more problems and the cycle continues.

I got caught in this cycle all throughout my teenage years. Alcohol was slowly killing me, but I could never get enough. I should have talked to someone about my struggles, but instead I kept drinking. And then, it was too late…

WOKE UP FROM A BLACKOUT

I woke up from a blackout going 140 mph.

I remember being ready to crash. Not because I had lost control, but because I wanted to. I was ready to leave this earth, ready to go because I felt like I didn't matter. I was tired of putting on a mask, tired of hurting, and tired of my alcohol abuse.

One bump, one divot, one wrong move and I'm gone—car flipped, life over.

The next thing I knew there were red and blue lights behind me. I was getting pulled over. "Maybe I should speed up faster and try to get away," I said to myself. And so, I did just that.

I started to speed up and tried to find a road to turn on. No such luck. There was nothing but highway ahead. But my never give up mentality kicked in.

I turned the car around and started heading the other way—straight at the cop car.

I wish I could tell you there was an epic shootout or a high-speed chase, but that would be a lie. The little angel of my subconscious told me to cut the act and pull over. So, the white flag went up and the chase ended. Anti-climactic, I know.

Due to my illicit behavior, multiple charges could have been pinned against me. Reckless driving, driving while intoxicated, and an attempt to flee the scene. However, all I was charged with was a DWI.

For the next eighteen hours, I spent my time behind bars. I slept on a thin blue cushion on the concrete floor, used the toilet with a cellmate watching, ate cold cornbread, baked beans and ham, and prayed that someone would pick up my collect calls.

It was an awful experience, but even worse was my mindset.

The only thing I wanted to do in that moment was drink.

Alcoholism is a disease that had captivated my mind. My dependency on it was so severe that I felt crippled without it. I can recall a time my parents found my alcohol in my room during high school.

As a punishment, they made me pour out the entire bottle down the sink in front of them. As ridiculous as this sounds, having to do this was one of the most difficult things I'd ever done in my entire life up until that point. I had such a dependency on alcohol, getting rid of the little I had was like getting rid of a piece of me.

I had an attachment to drinking. Alcohol was my friend, my buddy, my supporter, and my crutch. Without it, I'd fall. The more trouble alcohol got me in, the more I'd want to drink. But the more I drank, the more my problems were amplified.

It was a deceptive cycle.

NOVEMBER 14TH, 2019

After my DWI and three years of sobriety, on November 14th, 2019, I reopened a chapter in my life that I had worked so hard to previously close. Standing face to face with the skeletons in my closet was something that I didn't have the guts to do for years.

Knowing how far I'd come and how much I'd grown was one of the only reasons I was able to reopen this chapter of my life and take a step back in. I also knew that it wouldn't be right for me to ignore what once held me back from achieving all that is great in my life now.

For the sake of saving the trouble and maybe even the lives of those following me, I believe it necessary to add this very real account of my issues with alcoholism.

Haunted by demons and scared for my life, this is the first time I reread these accounts since they took place. Join me on this journey back to my darkest hour:

> *"If you don't stand for something, you'll fall for anything."* – Alexander Hamilton

Confessions of a kid lost in life:

Lord help me

Our Father, who art in heaven, hallowed be Thy name; Thy kingdom come Thy will be done on earth as it is in Heaven. Give us this day our daily bread; and forgive us our trespasses as we forgive those who trespass against us; and lead us not into temptation but deliver us from evil.

Lord help me.

Amen.

Journal entry from 2016 as I was still abusing alcohol:

11/14/16

It just seems like there is more sadness in the world than there is happiness. Too many people have died recently, and I've seen some of my friend's way too damn depressed. Getting a call and hearing the words, "I can't take it anymore. I want to kill myself," makes me question what sick, messed up "God" would give humans the ability to experience such pain. Then again, I must be honest too. I know the feeling.

It all started when a certain something started to create problems in my life. A certain something that made me feel on top of the world, until it didn't— alcohol.

Drunkenness, man, what a feeling. Confidence, laughter, dancing, social enhancement, and pure happiness. Nothing out there that can match the endorphin overload.

The first time I drank was sophomore year of high school. I thought I was cool. I thought I was the man. If only then would I have known that alcohol would ruin my life and bring suicidal thoughts upon me, I would have never started.

Nothing eventful happened that year besides a few parties. However, junior year was a whole different story. I should have never taken that first sip.

In the darkness of the storm that was about to ruin my life, a lighthouse stood clear in front of me. She shone brighter than a full moon and I would later find that she herself was Bill W. trying to help.

For the sake of her privacy, we'll name her Courtney.

Courtney was my best friend. She was and still is the most beautiful girl in the world. She had a heart full of gold and made me unconditionally happy, even without any alcohol in my system.

The first time I blacked out was junior year of high school. The second, third, fourth, fifth and sixth times as well. One might ask, "Why didn't you learn your lesson after the first time?"

My answer: I did learn my lesson after the first time.

But drinking was something I couldn't stop. I put it in front of the people I loved, the goals that I had, and the person I always wanted to be. I worried my poor mother and father, treated Courtney poorly, and lost the respect of my peers. It was a mentally defeating habit that I couldn't kick.

I pushed Courtney into a pile of bricks one night I was blacked out. I told her I didn't care about her another. I spit in her face and said things I still regret to this day. I ruined her Homecoming because I had to drink beforehand in order to have a good time. I drove her home while I was drunk so often that she would cry every time she got into the car. To no one's surprise, Courtney left me. And the light in my life went out.

But there was still one person I could fall back on. One person that I had known for so long. One person that I knew I could depend on when times got hard. There was no one like him. My best friend and dear pal, Mr. Alcohol.

I started drinking every chance I got. During the weekends, I never missed. Every Friday night I looked forward to it. I was hurt and disgusted with myself so I self-medicated with alcohol to mask my pain.

I started drinking excessively and making extremely dumb decisions. I'd steal from others, speed aggressively, mix alcohol with pills, call off work for weeks at a time so I could have more time to drink. I even went to school drunk—nearly every day for lunch I'd leave school to make a mixed drink just so I could get through my last classes of the day.

Alcohol turned me into a monster.

Junior year was slowly coming to an end. I was unhealthy, immature and in the adolescent stages of alcoholism. At just sixteen years old, I started to feel the first symptoms of withdrawal.

Irritable and restless mornings left me longing for a drink. Shaky hands and a short temper weren't uncommon for me after I woke up. I hid these symptoms from the people I loved because I didn't want them to know I was struggling. I didn't think things could get any worse.

Boy was I wrong.

The last day of junior year, my high school class went to the lake. I bought a full bottle of vodka all for myself. 750ML.

As a 6'2", 145-pound kid, I would be teetering on the brink of death if I were to drink the entire bottle myself. Yet, that was the plan. All but a few drops were left in the bottle by the time our forty-minute car ride had ended. The next twelve hours were a blur.

I still can't recall all the events that took place that day. I have been told many times over that I made a fool out of myself. The first incident being my drunken attempt to swim all the way across a crowded waterway of speedboats and pontoons.

The water was choppy, the boats were zooming by, and I was barely keeping afloat. With no life jacket on, the speed boats that raced by had little to no chance of seeing me. I was told that some boats weren't but a couple dozen feet from me.

The second incident was my dive into two feet of water in which I nearly broke my nose on a rock. As blood gushed out of my face, I stumbled uncontrollably out of the shin high water. My classmates were scared for me—others disgusted.

It wasn't long after this that I lay on the ground unable to get back up on my own two feet. My friends had to take turns fireman carrying me all the way back to the car. I threw up for hours. Then, somehow, I convinced my friends that I was okay to go home.

I walked right up to the front door of my house. Still blacked out and in no position to talk to my parents, I ran straight to the bathroom to clean all the vomit off me. Twenty minutes went by, then thirty, then an hour.

My parents couldn't figure out what I was doing. They yelled my name, pounded on the door. Nothing. They tried peeking through the window from the outside in. Nothing. Finally, they were able to pick the lock on the door and force their way in.

There I was, lying in the tub with water up to my chin, passed out completely.

My parents knew me well enough to assume that I was probably drunk. They tested their theory and yelled at me to get out of the tub. I resisted hastily. Unfortunately, the already chaotic day didn't stop here.

When my mother got me out of the bathtub, I started to run around my house. Completely naked. As I acted ridiculously, my family watched in disappointment.

"Here goes another one of Matt's drunken bits. When will he learn?" they must've thought.

This was a big wakeup call for me. Over the course of the next six months I cleaned up my act. I drank less, drank smaller portions, and did my best to be smarter about the decisions I made. As I slowly started to get a grip back on my life, things took a turn for the worse.

I went to Austin City Limits my senior year of high school. This was my favorite ACL ever. During the last performance, on the last day, Courtney and I fell back in love. I'll never forget looking over at her beautiful, brown eyes. Her welcoming smile made me melt. I knew this time it was real. She had my heart before, but this time she had so much more. I wanted to spend the rest of my life with this girl.

We were deeper in love than we had ever been. We spent nearly every second of every day together. We had our own special hammock spot and our own love for sunflowers. We loved full moons and Hallmark movies. We enjoyed swimming at the pool and wearing goofy goggles. We had dozens of sleepovers and shared thousands of laughs together. I took her to prom, and she took me to Boston to meet her family. She supported me, made me laugh and I finally felt right at home.

Those were the happiest seven months of my life.

Despite the perfect nature of our relationship, my drinking continued to get worse. This time it led me down a path of sure destruction. Clouding my judgment, alcohol struck again. Seven months of pure love and ecstasy was no match for my dear friend, Mr. Alcohol. I delve into temptation and acted upon my wandering eye.

Lust for a night is no match for eternal love.

I knew this, I kept this saying close to my heart. But the devil tempted me and temptation I took. Courtney was crushed and I couldn't ever possibly forgive myself.

When you hurt someone like that, you ultimately hurt yourself more. Sometimes it takes something as devastating as losing someone, to realize what's most important to you. I realized after I cheated that I had a serious problem. I had officially hurt all the people that were closest to me. I had no one left.

I lost all respect for myself. I felt empty and dark, so I drank. Then I drank again. Then again, and again. I could not manage without alcohol. I was hopeless and desperate for help. I no longer wanted to live. I was ready to die.

These thoughts were overpowering. Every time I drank, I felt as if I was being pulled closer to the fiery pits of hell. I felt misunderstood, and alone. Bad dreams made my nights unbearable. The sunrise filled my mornings with anxiety. My days were filled with fake smiles and fake laughs. I was restless, irritable, and discontent.

Alcohol brought me to my knees.

These are the last seven things I prayed for before finding help:

1) I am selfish and I need help.

2) I am inconsiderate and I need help.

3) I am quick-tempered and I need help.

4) I am greedy and I need help.

5) I am self-destructive and I need help.

6) I am an alcoholic and I need help.

7) This is why I must become sober. I need your guidance, Lord. Please help me make things right. Please help me change. I don't want to hurt anyone else; I want to be a better man.

Lord help me, then help me lead the lost souls.

CHAPTER 6

BREAKDOWNS CREATE BREAKTHROUGHS

In hindsight, I realize getting a DWI, spending time in jail, and losing the people closest to me due to my abuse, were the wake-up calls that I needed. It wasn't the best way to start college but these experiences helped me grow up. I may have been knocked all the way back to the starting line, but at least this time I was running in the right race. It allowed me to take the first steps in the right direction. I could finally start the rest of my life.

Still to this day, my battle with alcoholism has been a constant struggle. Every passing moment is difficult. Today is not easier than yesterday and tomorrow will not be easier than today. I genuinely work to take things one day at a time. It is the only way I can maintain my sobriety.

Occasionally I get asked if I regret giving up drinking during all of college. I understand why I get asked this. Yes, I did have problems with it then, but I could take a break for a few months now and be okay again right? The answer is no.

Alcoholism is a disease. You will always pick up right where you left off. If I were to drink again now, things would fall apart just as quickly as they first did.

Alcohol is like a long-time college buddy. After years apart, you get together, and things pick up right where they left off. It's as if things never changed. You guys still crack the same jokes, tell the same stories, and talk about the same people you used to hang around.

The same goes for alcohol. No matter how long it has been since you last drank, you will always be an alcoholic and always have the same relationship with your drink of choice. The same fun, the same excitement, and the same energy. But also, the same anger, the same instability, and the same problems.

I don't feel like I robbed myself of my college years by giving up alcohol. It was hard to think this way in the moment as all the fun was happening around me, but looking back, I know my decisions helped me get ahead.

It wasn't always easy, but I'm better for it now. I saved lots of time, trouble, and money. I was able to graduate college debt-free and the lessons of discipline I learned, will forever be rooted in me.

"Growth comes at the point of resistance". – Josh Waitzkin

27

THEN WHY DID YOU START?

I've been fighting personal demons my whole life. Despite having a wonderful childhood, I continued to tell myself that I was disadvantaged. I told myself that I didn't have it as easy as other kids or that things weren't handed to me.

This might have been the case, but I was still choosing to look at everything through the wrong lens. Instead of gratitude, I created this idea in my mind that I had it hard, that I was different, and that others wouldn't understand my pain.

This feeling of disconnect never went away.

As I got older, I realized that I created this false reality because I craved attention. I convinced myself that I had a tough upbringing when in truth, it was actually quite good. Yes, my family was a little different because I had a dad that was paralyzed. But it wasn't drastically different.

My overall health was great, we were financially secure, my quality of life was high, and our house was rooted in love. Aside from a few differences, my upbringing was about as normal as normal gets.

At the time, I did not have enough life experience to have the wisdom to realize this. This led to me creating a reality in my mind that wasn't completely true. Feelings of self-doubt began to grow because of my dad's disability. I felt judged, I felt less than, and it was hard for me to accept that being a little different was okay. So instead, I chose to put up a guard and act as if it didn't bother me.

As time went on, I became more and more insecure. The only way I could feel good about myself was if I could make others like me.

I was dying to get attention.

Alcohol was a way for me to feel more secure and silence my shyness. Drinking allowed me to quite the noise in my own mind. It helped me navigate the hardships of life on my own because I didn't feel like I had the mental strength to do it alone. I clutched to alcohol hard and created a crippling dependency. I felt like I could never get enough.

Addiction is a dark and lonely place. The only way to feel better is to consume more of that drug or substance, which makes you more addicted, and then the cycle continues. It's a never-ending loop, a never-ending struggle. You keep it a secret from others because you are embarrassed but in actuality the people you're hiding your addiction from are the people you need to tell, so they can help you find the treatment you need. You can't do it alone.

I used to hide full handles of alcohol in the back of my old electric keyboard organ so that I could drink while I did homework or before I went to hang out with friends. I used to hide beer cans in cabinets because I knew when the party went dry, I'd be upset and get short tempered. I'd steal drinks from people at parties because it would mean I could reach my preferred level of intoxication without having to get into my personal supply, which again, I knew I'd need by the end of the night.

I was willing to drink no matter how bad it got—passed out, broke, dead, or dumb.

I became an alcoholic because I was addicted to escape. Escape from my insecurities, my doubts, and my low self-esteem. Escape from boredom and escape from the thoughts in the back of my head. I was running away from myself because I didn't love who I was. If I would have kept going like I was going, I would have ended up in jail or dead.

The grind saved me.

"Everyone has a chapter they don't read out loud." – Unknown

WE'RE NOT THAT DIFFERENT

I'm not an old man telling you these stories. I'm barely twenty-two. I'm not that much older than you. I was in your shoes just a few years ago. I know what it's like to be where you're at. There is a lot of social pressure and it's hard. But I promise you, if you decide to make a change right now, it will be worth it.

If it's hard for you, it's surely hard for others too. So, be there for someone. Don't let a day go by without telling someone you love them. Check in on those that are hurting. Everyone is going through something and you might be the person that makes the difference and saves their life.

I guarantee that there is someone you know that is dealing with these same issues. Openly or secretly, alcohol or drugs has its grip on someone you love. This person can be an old timer, this person can be middle aged, or this person can be young like I was. I guarantee you someone is struggling.

"Help yourself by helping others" – John Templeton

The unfortunate part of this is that society undermines anyone with a problem. Lots of people out there are suffering in silence due to fear of embarrassment or because it's considered "weak" to go to others when you need help.

But it doesn't have to be this way. Don't suffer any longer. Don't be a prisoner in your own mind. Instead, be transparent about your problems, share your struggles with people you love, and always find someone to talk to.

Be an open book—vulnerability is the strongest thing you can do.

The happiness and clarity you will feel when you sober up is overwhelming. The selfish and narcissistic tendencies will go away. You will finally genuinely care for others and the beautiful things in life that surround you. You will feel happy and content. You will want to make others happy. And most importantly, you will feel part of something greater than yourself: a sense of belonging.

The love and acceptance you will feel from others after opening up about your substance abuse is unlike anything you've ever felt before. No grudges, no hate, no judgment. Just love and understanding.

Without drugs or alcohol, you'll be unstoppable.

"Everything you do is either leading you away from the masses or leading you away with the masses." – John C. Maxwell

Through my addiction, I learned that alcohol and other substances can and will hold you back. Sobriety is a luxury. You save money, time, and energy. With this extra money and time, you will gain clarity. And with more clarity, comes more freedom.

Sobriety allows you to experience things organically. You will remember the conversations you had, the jokes you heard, the people you caught up with. The stories that were told, the friends you saw, the music you danced to. No liquid courage needed. Instead, pure, organic connection.

I'm not saying all of you are blackout alcoholics or speech-slurring drug addicts. However, drugs and alcohol do have an adverse effect on the mind and body. Even in moderation, the chemical balance of your brain can be thrown off.

Sobriety gives you a chance to be genuine with people. Alcohol tends to make people act selfishly. Decision making becomes irrational, aggressive, and abusive behavior is common. So is irresponsible, neglectful, and illogical thinking.

People are afraid to give up alcohol, marijuana, and nicotine. Afraid it will change their social life or the way they will be viewed by their peers. But it does not have to be this way. You can still go out, you can still spend time with your drinking buddies, and you can still enjoy life. The only difference is that when you're sober, you can be in control.

Substances don't have to run your life. They don't have to consume you. Substances don't have to control your weekends or your weeknights. They don't have to be something you fall back on every time you're stressed, upset, or angry. You don't have to use substances as your crutch. You don't need to use substances as a safety blanket.

Once you come to the realization that substances don't truly benefit your overall wellbeing, it becomes easier to break free. But first, acceptance must take place.

"The pain of every change is forgotten when the benefit of that change is realized." – Tony Robbins

MY ACE – THE GIFT OF LONG SUFFERING

Once I accepted that I was an alcoholic, it was easier to change. One way that I've been able to maintain my sobriety is through a philosophy I created with the help of my good friend, Cody.

Sobriety is my ace. I can win any hand with it, including the hand of life.

If you think about it, we all have an ace: the highest or the lowest card in the deck. Depending on how you play your ace, you either win the game of life, or lose the game of life.

The Lord gave me a second chance. With this second chance, I promised myself I would right my wrongs and wouldn't ruin this new beginning. So, I played my ace to my advantage and my wins have brought me here, writing this book, to share my experiences and my story with you. My hope is that you won't make the same mistakes I did.

Sobriety is my ace. What is yours?

"Don't waste your pain—it's a useful paint." – Shia LaBeouf

PICK UP A BOOK INSTEAD OF A DRINK

I am now officially four years sober. Not even one sip of alcohol. And to be honest, I feel more present and focused than I ever have in my entire life.

I finally have a true sense of control and clarity. When I was at my rock bottom, I realized there was only one direction to go: Up. It was my chance to redeem myself, my chance to change, and my chance to make an impact on the world.

"I used that second chance to be a better man." – T-Pain

Sometimes in order to change the world, you need to change yourself first. Anyone can change. Anyone can make an impact who wants to. I don't care where you were at the end of high school or at the start of college. I don't care if you had gang affiliation or if you were addicted to drugs. I don't care if you were terribly shy or incredibly insecure. I don't care if you abused alcohol or partook in illegal activity. I don't care if you ruined relationships or destroyed family ties. None of these take away from your potential to be great. None of these things take away from your potential to make a difference.

Every one of you reading this is special and you can make an impact if you just believe in yourself. Put your past behind you and focus on the now. Focus on what is ahead. Focus on how hard you can work to make up for all the trouble you caused or the hardship you endured.

This book is for anyone and everyone who is willing to work hard and willing to change. This book is for anyone who wants to graduate college debt-free. I'm here to help you do that, but you have to promise yourself that you will put forth the effort, you'll put in the work and you'll follow the guidelines of this book.

I pushed myself during college to try and make up for the pain I caused not only myself, but other people during my wilder days in high school. I tried to make up for all the negativity I put out into the world. I wanted to change my influence, the nature of my sound and the frequency I put out into the universe. Looking back, despite being the hardest, college was also the best four years of my life.

I felt a sense of purpose. I knew I was working towards something greater than myself. This journey was the most beautiful thing that I ever experienced because I knew when it was all over, I'd be able to share my story with others.

Now that you know more about me, it's time to get into the good stuff. The rest of the book will be me teaching you how to use the power of your mind to push harder, how to accomplish anything you set your mind to, and how to overcome addiction, pain, and struggle.

Attempting to graduate from college debt-free might be the greatest challenge you ever face in your early life. But you will be surprised as to what you're capable of. You are amazing, you are powerful, and you will come out of this better than you started.

"Your attitude determines your altitude. It's not what you go through, it's how you go through it." – Zig Ziglar

CHAPTER 7

THE PARTY LIFESTYLE IS OVERRATED

Partying is fun. I get it. Trust me, I really do. Late nights out with your friends are always a good time. Not only that but they're also a great way to decompress and forget about the troubles brought with the work week, family, and school.

School and work can make life so monotone that going out and having a couple drinks with friends is the only way to keep your mind clear, the only way to spice things up and the only way to not be, well, boring.

Nobody likes the person who stays at home on their couch on Friday and Saturday nights. We all know that one person who seems to never be down to have any fun. They don't have the slightest bit of spontaneous, "live a little" personality in them. It seems as if you could offer them a million dollars and they still wouldn't go out. We all know someone like this, but we don't always know why they truly stay in, why they truly choose not to go out, and why they seem to always be so lifeless?

HOMEBODY, HOME HOBBY

That homebody was me. By choice. I usually stayed in for four reasons.

Number One:
The first being I didn't want to spend money. The more I stayed in, the less I spent on unnecessary things. The less I spent, the more I saved and the closer I got to graduating college debt-free.

The hardest part about reaching your goals is keeping the end in mind. However, if you're not able to visualize the feeling of achieving the goal you set out to accomplish, you'll get discouraged during the process of getting there. One of my favorite visualization techniques is the phone call technique.

Close your eyes and imagine that you're getting a phone call from the university you attend. You pick up the phone and answer. On the other end, the person is congratulating you. You just passed all your courses and have officially graduated. On top of that, they're notifying you that your final payment just went through, and you have no outstanding balance with the university. In other words, you've graduated debt-free. You hang up the phone. How does it feel? What emotions come across you? Who is the first person you tell?

You can do this technique with any goal. By keeping the end in mind and visualizing how it feels when you've accomplished your goal, you're putting yourself on a higher level of frequency. As long as you put in the hard work and continue to believe, the universe will remove obstacles that may get in your way and put things in front of you to help you get there—higher paying job, more ambitious friends, extra supportive family.

"What your eyes see, and your ears hear is what is already in your mind. As you think, so you shall be." – Harry Houdini

Number Two:

The second reason I stayed in was because of work. Most Friday, Saturday, and Sunday mornings were the days I made the most money. These shifts brought in the most tips; UT football games, Members Only Wine Tastings, and Shows at Bass Concert Hall in Austin, Texas. I couldn't risk sleeping through my alarm or showing up late to one of these shifts because of how lucrative they were. More partying often meant more shifts missed which meant less money earned.

During the 2019-2020 football season, Joe Burrow and the bayou boys from Louisiana State University came to Austin to take on Sam Elingher, Tom Herman, and the Texas Longhorns. This was a big weekend of work for me since I knew I'd be working as a valet on the day of the game, which hosted more than 100,000 fans in and around the stadium. On top of this, I planned to chauffeur on the Friday before the game, bartend a UT/LSU party that same night, then work a wine tasting event that Sunday. I never imagined I'd make as much as I did...

Instead of going out to the lake with my friends that Friday during the day, I chauffeured and made $210. Instead of going to Sixth Street that night, I bartended and made $490 and instead of going to the game that very next day, I valeted and made $225. Valet ended just in time for me to get off so I could go out and party but instead I picked up a shift for the very next day at a wine tasting event and made $200. I walked out that weekend making $1125. Sometimes being the homebody isn't so bad after all.

Number Three:

The third reason I stayed in was because of school. If I went out on a Wednesday night and missed class on Thursday morning, chances were I wouldn't find the time to relearn the material taught during that morning session. I was so busy already juggling multiple jobs and dealing with family matters at home, that I didn't have any extra time. That is, if I wanted to sleep of course.

This meant that the more classes I missed, the further behind I would get, and the higher chance I'd fail. I couldn't afford failing or dropping even one class if I were to graduate debt-free. Dropping classes meant adding them to later semesters and if I wanted to graduate early this couldn't happen.

My sophomore year of college I showed up late to class the day an essay was due. I had been out late with my friends the night before and didn't think it'd be a problem the next morning.

Despite having finished the essay weeks before the due date, I waited until the last second to turn it in, the day it was due. I walked to the front of the classroom to put my essay on top of the pile of other essays on my teachers' desk. As I was laying my essay down, my teacher slid her hand over the top of the pile and said, "You're late. I will not accept that essay." I tried to negotiate with her but saw that my efforts were pointless. She wasn't going to budge.

I visited her after class and tried to make up a story the best I could, but she could see right through the lies. I even went through the trouble of making a fake doctor note to excuse my lack of punctuality. These efforts were to no avail.

I passed that class on a Hail Mary good grade on the last test of the year, but it certainly wasn't worth the stress. What did I learn? Don't stay out late on a school night unless you absolutely have to. I never did it again.

Number Four:
The last reason I stayed in was due to self-improvement. Staying in on the weekends gave me the freedom to focus on myself. As everyone was out partying, I was inside reading about investing, healthy diets, philosophy, and psychology.

I'd be lying if I said I didn't wish I could get some of those nights back I missed a lot of parties, birthdays, holidays, and memories that I'll never be able to get back, but I believe it was worth the sacrifice.

I knew what my end goal was, and therefore I built up the willpower to learn how to say no. I continued to look past it all to keep the bigger picture in mind. I knew that those three to four years of college did not compare to the sixty years that lay ahead. I had to buckle down now, focus on my priorities, and learn to be okay with staying in. No parties. No bars. No late nights.

CAN'T BEAT THE TEMPTATION?

I don't expect all of you to be as obsessed with graduating college debt-free as I was. I was overly disciplined, overly frugal, and overly mundane at times. However, if you can't fight the urge to go out to the bars with your friends, or to parties with your classmates, this section is for you.

If you plan on going out to the bars or a party to get drunk, *pre-game first*. Go to the liquor store and buy yourself a pack of beer, cheap wine, or cheap liquor. Drink until you're content. THEN go out.

People will go out to the bars and buy drinks that are three times as expensive as the ones they could have bought and drank at their pre-game. If your drunk wears off, then settle for one of the cheaper drinks on the menu. I realize a vodka sprite or a vodka red bull tastes better than a cheap beer, Chad. But alcohol is alcohol, and if you're trying to save money then forget the fruity expensive drinks.

If this still breaks your bank, then go out sober. You may ask, what is the point of going to the bars if you're not going to drink? Well, to socialize of course. Sounds crazy, but you can hang out with friends and meet new people sober. Yes, you'll be a unicorn but who cares. It's always good to try something new, right?

The money saving aspect of going out sober is nice of course, but more importantly, there are no hangovers, you have more control over your decisions, you remember the conversations that took place, and you are more aware of your surroundings. I don't think any guy is fond of reflecting on a night that consisted of fighting a girl, peeing on strangers in an elevator, or nearly getting a public intoxication charge. Not that I've ever been around someone like this myself...

But again, going out sober allows you to think clearly. You can drive yourself home safely at any point which saves money since Ubers and Lyfts are pricey—especially on a Friday or Saturday night in a big city or during the weekend of a festival.

When you go out sober and give your friends a safe ride to and from the bars, you are not only saving money, but you might even make a couple bucks if your friends are nice enough to throw you some cash for helping them out.

THE MIND & BODY

Outside of this, drinking isn't the healthiest hobby. Everything in moderation is fine. Red wine is actually good for you when you moderate the intake. However, sober living is great for the body and mind. Slowing down on the drinking will help you lose weight, stop the early aging, and save your liver. You know, the thing in your body that stores excess carbs and proteins while also removing waste products and toxins. Kind of important to take care of this guy.

Additionally, the sharpness and mental clarity that comes along with giving up alcohol can create a whirlwind of positive habits that follow. With an extra sense of control over your body, your decisions and mind can become more powerful. This doesn't just stop at alcohol.

Narcotics, stimulants, depressants, and psychedelics not only cost money by physical purchase, but they cost money when your health is in shambles later in life. It cost money because you're spending time putting bad into your body rather than spending time putting good in your body like reading books, trying a vegan diet, learning how to knit, meditate, or do a magic trick so you can impress the girl working the window at the Arby's drive-thru. Be proactive!

CHALLENGE: Give up drinking, smoking and partying for thirty days. Do you feel refreshed? Have you filled your extra time with new, empowering habits? Have you been more productive? Have you saved more money? I bet you'll be able to answer yes to all these questions. If so, share your story on social media with the hashtags #gettingahead and #ultraproductive.

GREEK LIFE

Sororities and fraternities have lots of benefits. There is no denying this. The connections, networking and lifelong friendships created are hard to top. Additionally, the philanthropy events, volunteering and fundraising that takes place to help the community is special. However, Greek life can be expensive. And if you're not in it for the right reasons, it is better to just save that money and cut your losses early.

At the end of four years, dues at large universities can surpass the total of a new car, a semester of tuition or a down payment on a house. If you have no problem making friends, can find other ways to socialize other than Greek life parties, cookouts and events put together by the chapter council, then maybe you should reconsider joining. If you have an extroverted personality, then Greek life might not be worth the hit to your back account.

I hear people say that joining Greek life is like paying to be a part of a clique. I can't say this is true because I was never in a fraternity. However, I can understand that it could look this way.

Before joining Greek life ask yourself these questions:

The Greek Life Check Box

- Is paying for new friends worth it?

- Is paying for parties and events that you might not be able to attend or might not have a good time at worth it?

- Is paying for alcoholic beverages that you could just purchase yourself at a cheaper price worth the extra cost on the dues?

- Is it worth paying money to go to twenty-five toga parties in a semester?

- After you graduated high school, were you excited to never again have to see big shirt wearing, Starbucks drinking, Birkenstock Becky?

If you answered no to the first four bullet points and yes to the last one, then you really need to sit down and think about what worth your time and money before you rush. You don't have to be in Greek life to be considered cool. You don't have to be in Greek life to make lifelong friends. You don't have to be in Greek life to get a good job after college. You don't have to be in Greek life to have a good college experience.

PARTY FOUL

When did college become more about going out and partying and less about working hard and studying?

My roommate in college told me a story one time about a guy he let stay over at his place for a couple weeks to help him get back on his feet. He had recently lost his job and just needed someone to give him a chance. So, like the kind person my roommate was, he agreed to let his friend couch surf for a couple weeks if he agreed to be out by the end of the month.

As expected, these couple weeks turned into a couple months and by the end of the year the entire living room became a pig sty. There were dirty socks and underwear scattered all over the couch, left over fast food covered in mold, the sink was clogged, the trashcans were overflowing, and the dishes were piled chest high.

At this point my roommate had had enough. He told his buddy he'd give him a week to move out. The week went by and his friend claimed to have found a cheap place up the street in which he planned on moving into at the beginning of the next month. My roommate took his word for it and put up with him for a few more days.

Three or four days before finally moving into his new apartment the guy asked my roommate to borrow $50 and promised to pay him back. Assuming he was using it to pay for his weekly groceries or a partial down payment on his new apartment, my roommate gave the money with no hesitation.

My roommate came home from work later that night to see his friend on the couch with a bagful of marijuana. He was smoking a joint while dropping ashes all over the couch. Disrespectful? Definitely. However, what really pissed off my roommate was the fact that this guy had complained to my roommate that he was dead broke and had no money to buy dinner for the night.

The $50 he had given him was spent on weed when he very easily could have used that to pay for his meal that night. He chose to spend that $50 on the wrong things. Rather than on weed, he could have used the money to pay for appliances in his new apartment, gas for his car, or food for that night.

He fed on the crumbs of other people's hard work because he chose not to have his priorities straight. And to no surprise, when my roommate finally kicked his friend out, the guy didn't even have enough money to pay for a moving truck to get all the stuff he had moved in with.

Don't be this guy. Don't be the guy who doesn't have his priorities straight. Don't be the guy who always falls back on his parents to get him out of trouble rather than taking ownership of his own life. Don't be the guy who is too weak to turn down the need for a substance to make him feel sane again. Don't be the guy that promises to pay someone back but then never does.

If this person is you, it is time to change. It is time to right your wrongs and take full responsibility for the situation you're in. Start working harder and quit being a flounder-like bottom feeder.

If you are "broke" or having financial troubles, don't spend the first money you get on things that are not absolute needs. Money spent on wants, is money wasted when there are more important things that need attention. This is such an important thing to keep in mind.

There are so many college students who blow through all their hard-earned money because they don't have their ducks in a row. If you think this is you or could end up being you, start writing down your extra "unneeded" expenses on a piece of paper. How much do you spend on marijuana? How much do you spend on JUUL pods and vapes? Cigarettes? Alcohol? I will guarantee that most of you will be surprised to see the results.

Based on estimates I came up with after talking to friends and being an observer to their habits, this is what I came up with: JUUL pods, marijuana, and dab cartridges add up to $30 to $100 a week on the lighter end. That's $120 to $400 a month. Or $1440 to $4800 a year.

If you think these numbers are outrageous, then good, because they are. But this isn't far from what some kids between the ages of sixteen and twenty-four are doing. This doesn't even include alcohol and or cover fees for bars and clubs. This doesn't include getting food after a night of partying. This doesn't include dues for those who are in Greek life and this certainly doesn't include any trouble that one may get in while high or drunk in public or behind the wheel.

JUUL's, vapes, and dab pens are all money traps. You buy expensive oil, tanks, and E-juice. Next thing you know you're addicted to nicotine and it becomes even harder to kick the habit. Now, instead of smoking because everyone else does it, you're doing it out of necessity all throughout the day.

These are things you must think about ahead of time: "I never thought I'd get hooked," you might say. Nobody does, until they do. "I never thought I'd use it for this long," you might think. I don't think anyone just wakes up, buys a JUUL, and plans to smoke it for a set period of time. That's like saying you're going to register for a class to go just two months. Why sign up in the first place if you know you're going to feel guilty for dropping out? Same goes for JUUL's. Why buy one in the first place if you know it's not good for you?

"I promised myself I'd get rid of it, but I just couldn't." This is what happens, better just not to start in the first place!

41

"I'm not addicted, I could kick the habit, I just really don't see any problem with it!" If you could, then why haven't you? This just sounds like an excuse to me.

"I only hit it when I'm in the car." Until you don't. Next thing you know you're hitting it everywhere you go. It all starts innocently somewhere.

"I really don't use it that much." That's not the point, the point is you still have one and use it occasionally.

Whether it be a JUUL, a vape, a bong, or excessive amounts of alcohol, saving money is a commitment. If you want to graduate college debt-free you need to learn to prioritize. If you don't make saving money your number one priority and put it in front of everything you do over the course of the next several years, you will not graduate debt-free.

With that said, you can save a lot by not getting involved in these things. By setting your priorities straight, saving becomes easier. Moderating the partying and/or putting an end to it will pay you tenfold in the end. Putting harmful substances in your body never was and never will be cool.

For those of you who are mature enough to realize it, I salute you. For those of you who are just now learning this, welcome to the real world. And for those of you who refuse to believe it, you have a life full of trouble waiting for you!

Grow up and grow out of this phase and you will start to please your bank account. Those numbers will grow, and you'll be a happy camper. Keep tabs on how much you're spending on these things and you'll soon realize that I'm not making this up.

Don't spend your money on weed, invest it into a business. Don't spend money on JUUL pods, invest it into books. Don't spend money on alcohol, invest it into your mind. Do this and watch your life change.

CHALLENGE: Bring a notebook with you everywhere you go. Every time you spend money on questionable things, make a note of it. At the end of every week, tally all the money you've spent on nicotine, drugs, alcohol, fast food, and spontaneous purchases. Every week try and cut this cost by ten percent. The less you spend on these items, the more money you'll be able to put toward tuition and other costs associated with college. Are you surprised to see your results? Share what you discover on social media and include the hashtags #gettingahead and #ultraproductive.

BEFORE THE CRACK OF DAWN

My sophomore year of college I made a focus book. Inside the focus book, I jotted down bullet points and wrote down motivational one-liners to keep myself hungry. It was a way to channel my energy into something I could look back on during times I felt stuck. There were times I wasn't sure my sacrifices and hard work were really moving me forward. When I felt this way, I'd wake up before the crack of dawn and read those one-liners.

When the rest of the world was asleep, I could get my best thinking in. I'd sit at my desk and let the stillness of the morning put me in a tranquil frame of mind. After a few moments of complete peace and quiet, I'd open my focus book and get inspired all over again. These pieces of motivation kept me going when everything in my life seemed to be falling apart.

I think this is a great way to stay focused. I recommend you take the time to find quotes that resonate with you. Find quotes that speak to you on a personal level and write them down. Once you do this, you can draw inspiration from this focus book any time you're feeling unmotivated. These pieces of inspiration will keep you hungry and driven when times get tough.

Additionally, you can write down your dreams and goals so that you have a constant reminder of where you want to go. By defining exactly what it is you want to accomplish, you'll have a compass to follow. This sense of direction will keep you focused and accountable. Reflect, review and any time you are feeling unambitious, lifeless, or lost, you can pick up your focus book and dial back into the mindset that will help you take that next step.

CHALLENGE: Buy a journal or spiral notebook. On the front of the notebook, write 'Focus Book' in sharpie or a permanent marker. On the first page title it: Goals. Write down your one-month, one-year, three-year, five-year and ten-year goals. Be specific. Be detailed. Share your list of goals on social media and include the hashtags #gettingahead and #ultraproductive.

Once you finish this, go to the next blank page and title it: Rainy Day Quotes. Write down five of your favorite quotes. One quote for when you feel hopeless, a quote for when you feel discouraged, a quote for when you feel frustrated, a quote for when you feel unmotivated, and a quote for when you feel lost.

Then on the next page, title it: Better Day Quotes. Write down five more quotes. A quote for purpose, a quote for inspiration, a quote for motivation, a quote for never giving up and a quote for strength. You can draw quotes from this book as needed. There a plenty throughout this book that you can use at your disposal. However, I encourage you to find quotes tailored to your own personal story. Make sure they speak to you personally.

After you do this, go to the next page, and begin writing down positive affirmations. Let these flow out of you naturally. Below are pictures of how my focus book looked like when I was in college:

CHALLENGE: Write down your positive affirmations, quotes, and goals in your personal focus book. Share your list on social media and include the hashtags #gettingahead and #ultraproductive.

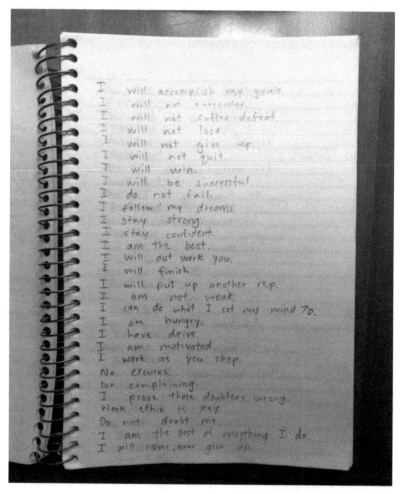

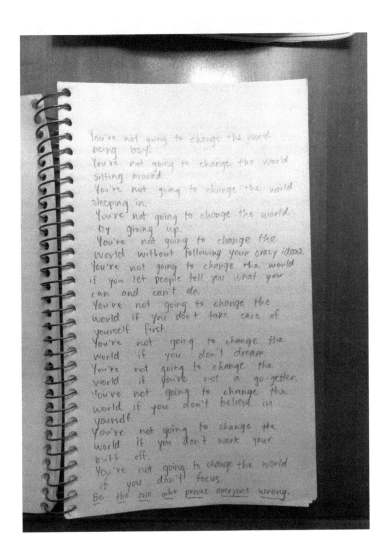

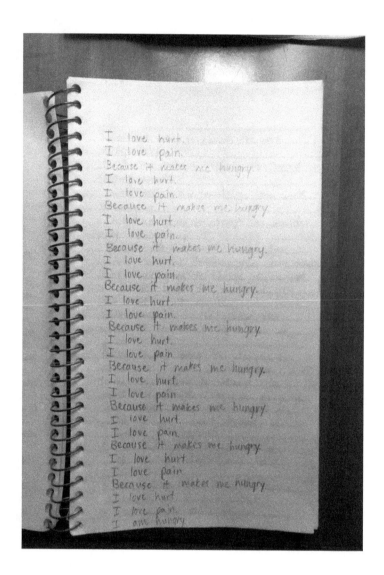

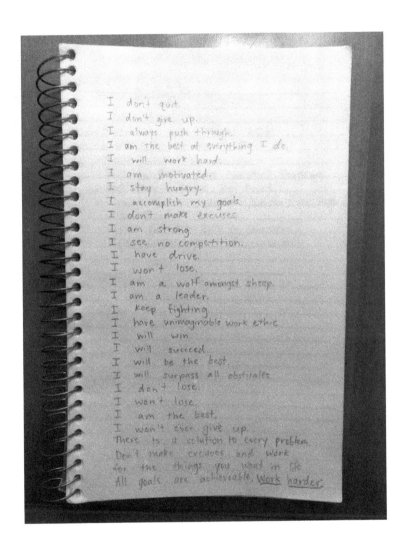

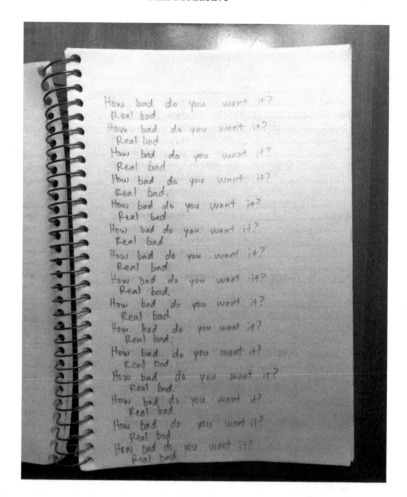

QUICK MOTIVATION

Don't be the person that posts motivational quotes and inspirational self-growth tips, then four hours later is guzzling Everclear and snorting cocaine like it's the 80s. Don't be the person who claims they're part of the "one percenters," working on themselves twenty-four hours a day, but in reality, is just sitting inside all day waiting to get out of the house to party. Don't talk the talk, if you can't walk the walk.

Quit eating late night Taco Bell and sleeping until two in the afternoon. Quit going to the bars when you promised yourself, you'd go to the gym. Quit spending money on clothes that you don't need just to act like you're some-one you're not. Don't preach a "motivational, go getter, do better lifestyle," if you're not living it yourself. And if you are at fault of any of this, remember one thing; Results speak for themselves. If this is you, sooner or later, you will get exposed.

Speak less and do more. Work your butt off and leave everyone else in the dust. Feel no mercy, no pity, no shame. You should never feel bad for working harder than other people. You should never regret late nights studying. You should never regret blowing people off to get one step closer to achieving your goals. You should never let turning down invites to make extra money, work on self-improvement or prepare for a test upset you. You don't owe anyone an apology.

Focus on yourself and what you're doing. Ignore the criticism and the doubt of others. You don't need reassurance, you don't need understanding, and you sure as hell don't need sympathy. All you need is the will to succeed, an unwavering belief that you'll make it, and a work ethic to back it all up.

"We are what we repeatedly do. Therefore, excellence is not an act, but a habit." – Will Durant

You know you've made it when other people start talking about all your wins and successes. People will wonder where it came from. It will catch them all by surprise. But this is what you planned. This is what you worked for. This is what you sacrificed for. This is what you dreamed of.

Everyone wants to claim they're the hardest working person in the room. Everyone claims they deserve it more. How are you going to differentiate yourself?

Work your tail off and challenge yourself every day. Write down your goals, track your progress and watch your dreams become your reality. Engage in consistent and watch as the life you've always wanted appears before your eyes. Graduating college debt-free will just be a byproduct of your unparalleled work ethic, unwavering belief of success, and unfazed discipline. To each their own.

"If you don't have a burning desire to better your life, you're cheating yourself and your loved ones with phony excuses. You're choosing a level of life that's poor compared with what you could have with the extra exertion you're capable of. It's all on your shoulders and there's no way you can shift a bit of the responsibility to anyone else." – Tom Hopkins.

CHAPTER 8

FLASHY LIGHTS, FLASHY CARS

Getting the flashiest of things and keeping up with the Joneses isn't always the best way to go about life. If you are overly insecure and care more about what others think about you than you do your own personal growth, happiness, and improvement, then you need to change. I'm not a physiatrist or a medical professional but I can say that isn't healthy. I won't lie to you either, loving yourself takes practice. But once you start caring less about what others think of you, the happier you will be. I guarantee it.

I used to have a 1998 Subaru Legacy. I had a love-hate relationship with this car. I loved it because I didn't have to get rides from my parents, but hated it because it was a hand-me-down with nearly 200,000 miles on it. For anyone who knows anything about cars, a car with this many miles has a lot of excess baggage. My Subaru Legacy, in particular, carried with it a list of problems longer than Santa's coal count on a Christmas night at Rikers Island.

In high school, I'd get off work at the movie theater at 5pm. As anyone living in a big city knows, 5pm is the peak of rush hour traffic. In Austin, you could be sitting in this road-rage filled congestion for well over an hour. As I would get closer to home, the sun would begin setting over the top of the highway overpass. This lighting pierced through the front windshield of the already frustrated drivers. Then there was me, my Subaru Legacy, and the worst twenty-five minutes of every day.

My Subaru would steam profusely from underneath the hood. The sun's rays would hit the front of my car at just the perfect angle, putting me, my Subaru, and the steam in the spotlight. The fumes would billow out from the front of my car creating a frenzy of drivers honking their cars at me to pull over. People would yell at me from out of their window begging me to jump out because they thought my car was about to explode.

As I pulled up to stoplights, people around me would be honking to try and get my attention. They would flail their arms at me, yell at the top of their lungs, and some would even get out of their car to tap on my window to let me know my car was fuming. As you can imagine, it was embarrassing.

Looking back, I'm surprised I put up with it for so long. I laugh about it from time to time and even share the story with others so they can get a kick out of it as well. It was a time I hope I never have to repeat, but I did it because

I was trying to save as much money as possible. I could have taken the bus or purchased a newer car but instead I chose to suck it up and save my money.

It ended up being a good move because once my senior year of high school came around, I was able to buy my own car outright. I walked in the Toyota dealership with sixteen grand cash and walked out with a 2015 Toyota Camry. Why a Toyota Camry? Let's talk about it.

TOYOTA, THE FERRARI OF THE SMART MAN

When purchasing cars, I recommend Hondas, Toyotas, and anything Hybrid. Hybrid cars are not only good for the environment, but they are also very fuel efficient. Not having to pay for gas will save you loads of money.

When I was in college, I watched a movie called *Gung Ho* and learned about Toyota's quality control procedure. This movie gave me a better picture of what Toyota's values are all about. There is a great amount of time and energy that goes into their attempts to create products that achieve near perfection. Toyota places an emphasis on durability, dependability, and long-lasting vehicles. I can confirm and advocate for Toyota that their cars last a long time. But if you don't have a Toyota or refuse to buy one, you can still make your car last longer if you take care of it the right way!

Don't be careless with your car. Wash it often, top off the fluids regularly, and drive safely always. Make sure your tires are filled to the recommend amount on the inside of the driver door. Check your spare tire and the tread depth in the other four. Don't leave your lights on after you get out. Don't try to park in tight spaces. Check for leaks once a month. Make sure your filters are clean and don't skip your routine checkups.

My neighbor, who was in the Navy, was the cleanest man I knew growing up. He would spend hours on his cars every day making sure they were spotless on the inside and out. I thought he was crazy for the longest time to be quite honest. But his Navy discipline paid off. To this day, he has kept his cars longer and in better shape than anyone I know.

I learned a lot of valuable lessons from his engagement in consistent action. He would always tell me the way a person takes care of their cars is a direct reflection of how they will take care of everything else in their lives. I took this piece of advice to heart and from that point forward always did my best to treat everything that I owned like the goose laying the golden eggs. You should too. Treat all your belongings like the golden goose. Keep them clean and keep them out of harm's way.

FRAME OF MIND

Flashy things = attention = a sense of superiority = a boost in ego and a silence to the underlying insecurity many of us feel.

It's okay to have nice things, but at twenty years old, is a $600 pair of shoes and a $70,000 car worth the temporary satisfaction of getting attention from your peers? A $60 pair shoes and a $7,000 car won't get you any special attention, but don't they fulfill the same purpose, getting you from point A to point B? They sure do.

The $60 pair of shoes provide the same heel support and protective capabilities as the $600 pair of shoes and the $7000 car gives you a quicker option of transportation, just like the $70,000 car. Both less expensive options do their job and get people where they need to go with no problems. So why continue to do otherwise?

Swallow your pride, tuck your tail, and put your ego aside. Eat a humble pie and save your money. Breaking the bank to have the flashiest of things won't provide you with the satisfaction you're looking for. This is only a quick fix to the deeper problems you're facing—seeking outward approval due to insecurity.

Humility is the key to keeping you working hard. Ego? That's the enemy.

This is a personal battle you will have to fight yourself. It will not be solved by irresponsible purchases. These things will not change the way you view yourself. These things will not heal the wounds from the past. These things won't change anything, except for the 0's in your bank account.

At this age, the best thing you can do is save your money. Learning this little discipline will prove to be much more valuable than any attention you get from buying a nice car, nice clothes, or a nice house. Barely scraping by because of the monthly payments you have, is not worth your extra time and energy. That is, extra time and energy you could be using to start building your kingdom of knowledge, security, and financial freedom.

I'm not saying you shouldn't buy nice things. All I'm saying is high dollar purchases at a young age aren't a wise decision. It is better to save this money and use it on something with higher importance—your college loans, investing in your Roth IRA, or buying a book about generating cash flow and passive income. I understand you've worked extremely hard and deserve to treat yourself occasionally, but high dollar purchases shouldn't be at the top of your priority list when you're trying to graduate college debt-free.

Speaking from experience, I guarantee that you don't have to have the nicest and flashiest of things to be happy. You don't have to keep up with the Joneses. All you have to do is keep your eye on the prize. Stay focused and don't allow yourself to get distracted in temporary satisfaction. Block out the outside noise, don't get your goals confused with what the rest of the crowd is doing and get to work. Now is not the time to be careless with your money.

"Control your urges now because the payoff will be much sweeter down the line." – Unknown

CAN'T ACCEPT THE RIDICULE? KEEP UP BUT SPEND LESS

If you are unable to comfortably take a step out of the limelight when it comes to clothing and style, there are still some options for you. Thrift shops, garage sales, second-hand stores and outlet malls almost always have high quality finds. Goodwill, Plato's closet, and various other thrift stores do their best to keep up with the latest fads and trends to keep their customers coming back. These stores keep up with the style that is currently in but sell their items at a much lower price.

I relied on these stores all throughout high school and college. Half of my wardrobe came from thrift stores. I bought dress slacks, winter coats, Nike shoes, Tommy Bahama shirts, Columbia shorts, Wrangler jeans, and Polo hats. I could spend cheaply while continuing to stay in style with name brand items.

You can spoil yourself at thrift stores since the prices are cheaper. I guarantee that you will always come across something you like. Not only that, but the price will be much more reasonable than going out to buy brand new clothes. These retail stores will allow you to stay within your price range and budget.

This goes for cars too. Don't be the guy that is making payments on a nice sports car but is living in a beat-up apartment or house. That just doesn't make sense. Cars are a depreciating asset. Live in an apartment or buy a house that goes up in value over time (if the market is right and city is growing of course). Start building equity, live below your means and save!

DON'T COMPARE YOURSELF TO OTHERS

You should be so focused on what you're doing that you don't have time to worry about what others are doing. My good friend, Sean, laid a quote on me my junior year while we were eating lunch at Thundercloud Subs, yes with a coupon, that ultimately changed the way I viewed things for the rest of my life. He said, "Comparison is the thief of joy"[2]. And it really is.

I thought about it for a while. I always thought of myself less than because I didn't have the fancy cars or the big house. I didn't take the fancy trips to the Bahamas, or to the French countryside to go on wine tours. I didn't go to Las Vegas, Nevada or Hollywood, California. I shopped at Old Navy rather than Lulu Lemon and took hand-me-downs from my cousins.

When shopping, I'd go straight for the clearance rack rather than waste my time around the sections in the mall that I knew I didn't have the money for. I never had the newest phones or latest video games. I either wore clothes that weren't in style or went to thrift shops to see if I could find the closest thing to it. My friends wore Calvin Klein underwear, I wore BCG. My friends had Nike Cleats, I had Rawlings. My friends wore Ralph Lauren button downs, I wore no name Plato's Closet pickups.

For prom, I didn't want my parents to pay for a tuxedo that I would only wear for one night, so I went to JC Penny, picked out the cheapest blazer I could find and bought it. Four years later, as a senior in college, I was still wearing that same $70 blazer at interviews, job fairs, and weddings. It was oversized then and still doesn't fit me now, but I sure have saved a lot of damn money with it.

I always felt like I had to work harder than others. I had to sacrifice a lot. Most of my weekends were consumed with double digit hours of work, weeknights were filled with playing catch-up on my homework and the rest of my free time was mostly spent at the gym trying to relieve stress. Birthday parties, graduation events, concerts, you name it. If you can list it, I had to miss it.

But here is the thing, it didn't matter. It didn't matter what everyone else was doing because I was creating my own path. Those long weekends and near sleepless nights-built character, resiliency, and grit.

Even then, I was blessed. My parents did a fantastic job providing. I grew up well and had support and love which a lot of people don't have. There was

---

[2] President Theodore Roosevelt

no point in comparing myself to others because that would have robbed myself of the things that I did have and all that was going for me.

If you do compare yourself to others, make sure you're doing it the right way. Sometimes knowing your differences is a good thing. Being different isn't always bad. It makes some people hungrier. I always felt a little different, so I began to use it to my advantage. My differences were my strengths. Each difference was another chip on my shoulder and other cookie in my cookie jar of inspiration, as David Goggins would put it.

I'd dig into that cookie jar when times got hard. I'd remember what separated me from others growing up and used that as fuel to the fire. I started to work harder and dream bigger. Resiliency and hunger grew within me and my determination to succeed got stronger.

Looking back, this switch in mindset was one of the greatest things that happened to me and one of the greatest things that will happen to you too. Using your differences as strength is exactly what you need to do. Use your shortcomings as motivation. Don't look for approval through materialistic things. Be you and be okay with that. You are enough.

"Behind your eyes is more important than what is in front." – Jonathon Carter

DON'T BE A VICTIM

Never forget you are the co-creator of your reality. What you speak into the world becomes your truth. What you believe on the inside manifests on the outside. Your reality is truly all in your head. This idea is the basis of all ancient wisdom schools.

Get up every morning and speak your affirmations aloud. Be absolutely certain you will accomplish your goals and begin getting ahead. These beliefs and this inner reality has the power to shape your outer reality. Speak your beliefs with confidence and certainty. Clear yourself from where you are, to where you intend to go. Whatever you have in your environment reflects your consciousness. Once you put the correct energy out into the world, it will manifest, and those ideas find you.

Inadvertently, your negative thoughts can do the same. Don't be a victim to your own mind. Your situation is not a punishment, it's an opportunity. The tough situations and downfalls you experience are leading you to something greater. Use your pain as an instrument to greater growth. Embrace the darkness. Own it, don't bury it. Live your life. Use your situation as fuel. Leverage the pain, darkness, and hardship to make you stronger and wiser. Suffering is a choice.

> *"When things aren't going your way, when things are not happening as fast as you want them to happen, don't blame everyone else. You're the reason your life isn't at the next level. Stop running around acting like you don't have a choice. You decided that those were your thoughts. You decided those are your friends, you decided those are the people you want to hang around, you decided that's what you wanted to do with your day. Feeling good isn't just an opportunity, it's a responsibility we have to make for ourselves."* – Tyrese Gibson[3]

SWALLOW YOUR PRIDE

Shortly after I graduated from college, my friends and I would do outdoor workouts at a track nearby our house. At the end of every workout, we were all exhausted.

One of these evenings, the five of us got a workout in more intense than anything we had done up to that point. Our legs were shaking as we tried to catch our breath.

Sweat dripped off our arms and face and we all laid down in the grass to try and recover.

All of us but my two friends, Dain and Brian.

During the midst of this fatigue, pain, and misery, Dain and Brian decided to continue running sprints up and down the football field. They wanted to push themselves to their limit, break their comfort barrier and go one more. It was a display of stoicism at its finest.

As Dain and Brian were mid-sprint, one of my friends laughed at them hastily. He looked over at the rest of us and said, "God damn try hards."

I couldn't believe it.

How are you going make fun of someone who is trying to get better?

To the friend of mine whom said these words: If you're reading this—I love you, man, but when you said that it revealed a deep defect in your character.

---

[3] https://www.youtube.com/watch?v=HSYiQWpmg-s&feature=emb_title

You're belittling people who are trying to get better. You were downgrading the fact that they were trying to grow. As you were sitting, giving up—they were doing more reps. You said what you said to make yourself feel better about being lazy.

I think about this memory from time to time and can't help but think about how it applies to so many different scenarios, like school, sports or work.

KISS UP OR MISS OUT

People criticize other people who are kiss ups, teacher's pets, or Yes-Man's. But it works, doesn't it?

These people are always the favorite of the teacher, coach, or boss. What does the favorite end up getting? Better grades, more playing time, and more money, right? So why bash on them?

Don't be so damn prideful. These benefits will slip through your hands if you let your pride get in the way. Sometimes you have to kiss up to get what you want. This is just part of the game of life.

When you were a kid, you did extra chores or made sure to act on your best behavior to get an extra piece of candy or money to spend at the ice cream truck. Yet, in life, you're not willing to put in that extra energy to get a second chance on a test, extra attention on the court/field or a raise at work. You put your pride ahead of success and achievement.

Now that's ridiculous.

Throw your ego aside and go kiss ass. Who cares what everyone else thinks? If it benefits you, it's worth it. Stay away from haters, that sh*t is contagious!

"Where our attention goes, energy flows." – James Redfield

CHAPTER 9

SURROUNDINGS MATTER

You tend to become most like the people you surround yourself with. If you hang around people that party every night, then you will be more inclined to do the same. Equally so, if you hang around people who are studious and stay in the library until sunrise, then you will do the same.

If you hang around people that spend freely because they come from families that are well off or haven't perfected their own spending habits, then you will begin to do the same. However, if you hang around those who are frugal with their money and work multiple jobs to save more, than you will do the same. It is extremely important to be aware of the influence your friends and those you spend most time with have on you.

It is always good to evaluate yourself and the habits of the people you spend time with. Don't let yourself get caught into peer pressure based simply on the fact that you don't want to be the odd ball in the group. Nor should you want to surround yourself with people that tend to peer pressure others anyway. Pay attention and attention will pay you. Set the right example, and others will follow.

Be the role model and set yourself apart from the crowd. Sometimes creating your own path is the best route to take. Different is good when it benefits you. This is your time to be selfish and not feel bad about it. You aren't tied down to a job, a spouse, or a set plan. You can create your own destiny. You can create the future you want. It's all in your hands.

Surround yourself with the right people. People that support your goals and aspirations. People that encourage you to freely experiment. People that inspire you to be good, do good, and focus on what is right.

Save your money and hang around people who are trying to do the same. Surround yourself with people that understand the value of a dollar. This might mean you have to start spending time around people that come from entirely different backgrounds and have entirely different stories. This might be intimidating but it is okay.

These are the people that will understand why you're trying to save. These are the people that it will be easiest to be around because of the similarities in character and lifestyle. You will find you have more in common with them and will be more comfortable. This will pay dividends in the long run because you will find yourself much happier.

By surrounding yourself with other people that are trying to graduate college debt-free while also achieving high levels of success, you will be motivated even further. You will feel more of the urge to climb because you are surrounded by people with similar attitudes. Collectively, you will all be striving for a higher quality of life.

"Show me your friends and I'll show your future." – Chaplain Ronnie Melancon

CHALLENGE: Reflect often and ask yourself these questions:

a) Are your intimate associates mentally superior or inferior to you?

b) Are your friends judging you or helping you develop?

c) Do your friends save more than they spend?

d) Do the people you associate with work more or less than you? Do they work harder or less hard?

e) How often do you talk about other people rather than discussing ideas and visions?

If the answer to these questions trouble you, it's time for a change. Be brutally honest with yourself and post on social media your own faults. Then list the character traits of the type of person you aspire to be and those you look for in others. Include the hashtags #gettingahead and #ultraproductive.

THE POWER OF ASSOCIATION

Once you start surrounding yourself with other people that shine with ambition, you will begin changing the way you see yourself. These people will lift you up and make you feel better every day. This hunger will increase your work ethic and boost your self-confidence. You will begin refusing to accept anything less than what you are worth: job, relationship, money.

This will give you the liberty to put your own price on the things you do for others. Those around you will begin to have more respect for you because of your confidence, alleviating any need to prove yourself. You won't settle for $15 dollars an hour if you know you're worth $25. You won't settle for the comfort of a relationship when you know you can do better. Once you respect yourself, others will begin respecting you too.

"When you have a million-dollar dream, don't let someone with a $30,000 salary talk you out of it." – Mentality

THE DILEMMA

I think we can all agree that life is more fun when we surround ourselves with the people we love. However, sometimes the people we love are the ones that hold us back the most. It's natural to cling onto someone when we can't keep up, but for the person going faster, we're slowing them down.

Have you ever raced a friend, family member, or stranger in a pool? When they started getting ahead, did you pull them back to pull yourself forward? The same happens in life. When you're moving fast, others try to pull you down because they can't keep up. This is tough because you know separating yourself is the best thing for you, but by doing so, you're leaving behind those you care about. This is never easy, but sometimes in life, in order to grow, you need to let go.

Have you ever heard the saying, "You hang around the barber shop long enough, you'll end up getting a haircut"?

Again, the same analogy can be used in life. If you surround yourself with successful people, you'll end up grinding and being successful. To get something you never had, you have to do something you never did. To get different, you have to do different and to do different you have to be different. Set yourself up for success and don't settle for less.

"High achievers don't like mediocre people and mediocre people don't like high achievers." – Nick Saban

FINAL THOUGHTS

Focus on yourself and forget everything else! You must leave the people behind that aren't doing you any good. The friends that only take and never give. The friends who don't have their priorities straight and are unorganized.

The friends who are addicted to comfort. Don't let the irresponsibility of others get in the way of your destined greatness. You need to keep only those that support your ideas and have ideas of their own to add.

Are they throwing pennies into your well or drinking from it?

The insecure and irresponsible want to hang around those who have it together because it makes them feel better about themselves. They want you to stoop to their level, so they don't feel bad for being the only one. Be a leader, not a follower. Don't get comfortable. Ride with your peers until they can't keep up. Slow down for no one. You are headed to greater places.

"Sometimes losing people helps you find yourself." - Unknown

WHAT KEEPS ME DRIVING

I didn't want to have any worries with my money once I got older. Therefore, at an early age I made a promise to myself that I wouldn't let anything stop me from climbing the ladder of financial success. You shouldn't either. Work your tail off, properly manage your finances, budget intensely, and everything else will fall into place.

A helpful approach for me was to look at everything long term. I thought about my future kids. I wanted to do everything in my power to set them up better than I had been. My grandma grew up on a dairy farm with seven siblings in a small town in Iowa. They would milk cows and pick eggs for breakfast. My dad had four siblings and worked in the family restaurant starting at the age of eleven. I started working at fourteen but lived in a house nicer than the one my dad grew up in—and much nicer than the one my grandma stayed at in that little Iowa farm town.

My dad broke his generational curse and I plan to do even better. I don't want my kids to worry about paying for their own college tuition. I don't want them to have to worry about car insurance or their rent every month. Do it so your kids don't have to. This is the end goal.

Set your family up and future generations to come.

The big wins can start with you.

CHALLENGE: What keeps you driving? What is the driving force behind all your hard work and aspirations for success? Once you figure out your

61

WHY, share it with the rest of the world. In a social media post, talk about your WHY with the hashtags #gettingahead and #ultraproductive.

CHAPTER 10

COMMUNITY COLLEGE IS THE HOLY GRAIL

Don't let anyone degrade or belittle you for going to a community college. Not everyone comes from the same financial background. Going to a community college was the best decision I ever made, and I am extremely proud to say I got my first degree from one.

With that said, for those of you paying for your own education, community college is the holy grail. Most cities, small or big, have a community college. If not in the city you live in, surely there is one nearby.

Community college is great for a variety of reasons. One of the best perks is the size of the classes. Community colleges tend to have a smaller student population. Therefore, the student-to-teacher ratio allows students to receive more one-on-one time with their professors. This extra attention improves individual performance and gives students the feeling that they are genuinely important in the eyes of the teacher.

Auditoriums at large universities can hold as many as 500 students. With this many bodies, it is nearly impossible for professors to make sure each student in the class understands the information that is being given. Also, with this many students, it makes it very hard for a professor and their teaching assistants to reply to emails in a timely manner, grade materials quickly, and hold struggling students accountable for their discrepancies.

At community colleges, professors have less students to keep track of. They can direct their attention more on singling out the individuals that need extra help, rather than trying to figure out how they're going to help hundreds of students at once. This makes students feel wanted and appreciated rather than "just another number."

Another great benefit of community college is that they provide people with a second chance to mature and grow. Students who didn't take high school seriously or couldn't make the grades to get into the school of their dreams, have a second chance to improve their GPA and reapply. Additionally, achieving good grades in a community college can help you earn scholarships that previously wouldn't have been available to you.

Furthermore, community colleges accept all—regardless of age, race, and background. Campuses tend to be extremely diverse and accepting. This atmosphere transforms lives and provides a comfortable learning environment. Community colleges are for anyone and everyone, providing an opportunity for all to succeed.

Typically, community colleges are made up of students with similar stories. Majority of the students work part time or full-time jobs and are trying to get an education while saving money. Since many students at community colleges work on top of taking classes, community colleges understand that their students need flexibility. Therefore, most offer more weekend and night classes than a regular four-year university would. If you need to work while in school or take classes that fit around your family's schedule, you'll have a lot more options at a community college.

SCHOLARSHIPS

Despite this being one of the most important sections of this book, I'm not going to devote much time on this topic. There are so many variables when it comes to scholarships, so I am just going to trust that each of you do your own research to find what scholarships fit you best.

I can't tell you the exact ones to apply for since they vary by GPA, state, institution, age, race, gender, time of year, type of major, combined household income, extracurricular activities, and many over variables. However, I can say that no matter who you are, you need to apply to as many scholarships as possible.

My older sister got nearly half of her college tuition paid for through scholarships. She made it a priority to apply for as many scholarships as she had time for at the beginning of every year—even the scholarships she was almost positive she wouldn't receive. She believed that some chance at winning a scholarship was better than no chance at all. Most of the time her applications would turn out in her favor and she would get one step closer to graduating college debt-free.

You can do the same! Instead of going to the movies or turning on Netflix, apply for a scholarship. Instead of going out to eat with your friends, apply for another. Make it your goal to apply for at least one scholarship a day. After three weeks of doing this, you've raised your chances of receiving free money. The more scholarships you apply for, the closer you also get to graduating college debt-free!

If you go to Austin Community College in Austin, Texas, make sure to apply for my scholarship. I award $2,500 yearly to a hard-working candidate. The next one could be you!

CHAPTER 11

HOME SWEET HOME

If I had the choice, I would have lived at home the entire three and a half years I was in college. Unfortunately, the closest school to accept my transfer application, after finishing my coursework at community college, was forty-five minutes away. I could have commuted, but my class schedule was scattered all over the place.

Since I was a transfer student, I was forced to sign up for classes later than all the other students. This meant I couldn't pick my own schedule the way I would have liked—leaving me with classes at varying times on varying days. It made it too difficult to commute back and forth so I found an apartment and moved in.

After this first experience of selecting my class schedule, I learned that there was a pecking order to the Texas State class registration system. Seniors signed up for classes before juniors, then sophomores, and finally freshman. I realized that if I were able to select my classes before they got filled up, I'd have a better chance of getting the schedule I wanted, and I'd be able to commute. I promised myself, come my senior year, I'd do whatever it took to make sure I got the best class schedule possible.

The beauty of commuting was that I wouldn't have to pay for an apartment again. Instead, I could park at my friend's apartment for free and take the bus to class. This would allow me to save over $700 a month on rent, while only having to pay $50-$100 a month for gas to commute. In total, it would cost me less to commute to campus every week for an entire semester, than it would have cost me to pay one-month worth of rent.

An ideal commuter's schedule for 15 hours of course work looks something like this:

- Monday's – OFF

- Tuesday's – 8am, 9:30am, 11am, 12:30pm, 2pm

- Wednesday's – OFF

- Thursday's – 8am, 9:30am, 11am, 12:30pm, 2pm

- Friday's – OFF

Whose schedule was this? This was my actual schedule my last semester of college. I had classes back to back to back for six hours straight, no gaps. This allowed me to get home early and spend the rest of my days making money, spending time with my family, or doing homework. By commuting just two days a week rather than four or five, I was able to spend my days off from school working full forty to sixty-hour weeks all throughout my final semester.

The reason I was able to get such an ideal schedule my last semester was because I refused to accept that being a senior was the only way to get priority selection status on registration day. I began to look deeper into the Texas State selection process, and sure enough, there was a loophole!

Students who achieved high levels of academic excellence at Texas State could be admitted to the Honors College. These bright individuals were given precedence when it came time to selecting classes for the upcoming semester. I knew that if I wanted to get my ideal schedule, I'd have to get admitted to the Honors College. During my entire junior year, I worked my butt off and before I knew it, I raised my GPA and qualified for the Honors College. But before I got admitted, there was still one more step. I had to go in for an interview.

The only way the Honors College would admit me was if I promised to continue meeting specific requirements throughout my tenure Texas State University. The requirements included: a 3.25 GPA, writing a thesis paper, taking additional course work per class and lastly, an hourly minimum. This is where things got tricky.

The Honors College required its students to graduate with roughly sixty hours of Honors College course work. By graduating from Texas State early, I would not have been able to meet the hourly minimum, but I also knew if I wanted to graduate college debt-free, I needed to get accepted. So, I bluffed.

The day of my meeting, I put on a poker face. When the admissions officer asked if my intentions were to graduate from the Honors College by meeting the listed criteria, including the hourly requirements, I stretched the truth and said yes. The bluff went unnoticed and I got admitted.

The following two semesters, I earned priority class selection status. This allowed me to choose the class schedule mentioned earlier in the chapter. Additionally, this schedule allowed me to work the hours in which I'd make the most money—and helped me commute from Austin without having to pay for another six months of rent.

If your school has an Honors College, look into applying. You might find that there are special benefits, just like I discovered at Texas State. If it helps you get one step closer to graduating college debt-free, then it's worth it.

TAKEAWAY

Living on your own can be a blast, but it is expensive. Personally, I spent close to $10,000 extra when I had my own apartment and was living away from home for the first time, than I would have if I continued living with parents. It was a complete lifestyle change. Being on my own gave me the freedom to do as I pleased but this wasn't always a good thing.

It's easy to get caught up in spending irresponsibly when the people you hang around do the same. Most of my friends got an allowance every week from their parents. This gave them the luxury to spend carelessly. I, on the other hand, didn't have the means to do this, but I tried to keep up.

If you want to live away from home or don't have the choice to commute, sign your lease early. Get on the ball as soon as you possibly can. Apartment complexes have early sign on bonuses and deals when you commit early on. These deals include cheaper monthly rent, waived housing deposits, visa gift cards, gaming systems, and many more great gifts.

Additionally, make sure you sign into a lease that is yearlong. Anything below that, is terribly expensive. It's rare being able to find a six-month semester lease that's affordable. Semester leases are generally more expensive per month.

With that said, commuting is still a more affordable option. It isn't always fun living at home, but you can't forget the end goal. In order to graduate debt-free, you have to make sacrifices. If it were easy, everyone would be doing it!

RESIDENT ASSISTANT

Another effective way to save money on rent and housing expenses while in college is becoming a Resident Assistant (RA). Resident Assistants at most colleges get their room and board paid for. They get put in a dorm room for free, receive a meal card, and only work a couple hours a week in return. This is a huge win if you don't have a car or any form of transportation to get to and from a job outside of campus. RA's save thousands on their housing and meal plan every year.

Year leases for apartments, condos, and houses typically run about $7,000 to $14,000. This number is influenced heavily depending on the quality of the place you live in, the number of roommates, and the extra amenities. Food and rent are usually the two largest expenses. Therefore, becoming an RA is a great way to eliminate both headaches.

Combined, RA's can save anywhere between $15,000 and $75,000 on food and rent during a typical stint of three-years. For most schools, this is over a year's worth of college paid for—in full, with all living expenses included. Additionally, if you decided to go to a community college first and managed to pay for your tuition in full while enrolled, then transferred to a larger university afterward, all you would have left to worry about is one to two years of tuition and fees.

This is a totally manageable number if you take advantage of summer classes and/or use the extra time during the summer to pick up a job. Working a few jobs in that three-month period can have a significant impact on paying for your tuition and possibly even cover the cost altogether.

Here are personal accounts from my older sister, Lindsey Worthington, and friend, Logan Taylor, regarding their experience in college as Resident Assistants:

LINDSEY WORTHINGTON

There are a lot of benefits to being a Resident Assistant (RA). At the top of the list was the opportunity it gave me to have a positive impact and influence on my residents. During my time as an RA, I was able to network and gain exposure to different people and cultures. This helped me learn how to better understand my residents and cater toward their varying needs. By doing so, I was able to make some of my closest friends, many of whom I still keep in touch with and see often.

As an RA, we received a lot of useful training that helped me hone my interpersonal and leadership skills. We received various trainings including Ally, QPR (suicide prevention), diversity and inclusion. We also learned about communication and leadership styles which in turn allowed me to improve my leadership abilities. These trainings helped me become not only a more effective RA, but also proved to be powerful in my personal life as well.

Financially, most of my costs associated with college came from my freshman year, in which I paid for housing and tuition on my own. After sophomore year, when I became an RA, my only expense was for my tuition. I was able to get my housing paid for, a meal plan, and a stipend every two weeks. This allowed me to save money, make money, and ultimately, graduate debt-free, which has been a huge stress relief going into graduate school.

Looking back, being an RA was a very positive experience. It was not always easy, or a walk in the park; but in the long run, it was definitely worth it and paid off. I wouldn't trade my time as an RA for anything.

LOGAN TAYLOR

Being an RA was one of the highlights of my undergraduate experience. During my year and a half of being in this position, I made some of my best friends and created memories I'll remember for a lifetime.

Being an RA can often feel like a draining task just to get free housing, but in my opinion, it is what you make of it. Don't get me wrong—it isn't always sunshine and rainbows, but it is worth it. During my time as an RA, I got to meet so many amazing people, many of whom I keep in touch with, to this day.

From a financial perspective, being an RA helped me out so much. A lot of my current student debt comes from my freshmen year, purely from being required to live on campus. Five years later, I still remember the financial impact of that first semester, the relationships and experiences made. However, once I became an RA, I was able to save thousands of dollars which in turn helped me graduate with less debt.

Lastly, being an RA was wonderful because of the impact I was able to make on others. Knowing I helped young adults through one of the most exciting, yet difficult, transitions in their lives was powerful. I didn't know I had the ability to touch the lives of as many people as I did. Knowing that I made a difference is all the reassurance I need when debating whether my time as an RA was worthwhile.

CHAPTER 12

THE ART OF FRUGALITY

Being frugal is an art. No one is just born with the desire to save. Naturally, humans have the want for more, a lust for the best money can buy and an attraction to luxurious lifestyles.

Dreams of the rich and famous.

Red sports cars, a big house, and endless travels.

But being frugal takes time and practice. It is an art that must be learned and rehearsed. Some of us were lucky enough to have parents who instilled this mindset and lifestyle in us at an early age. However, the craving for more can be overpowering if not properly handled. In order to truly become frugal, you must commit to the art daily. It must become part of your personality and it must be practiced often.

Let me give an example: I think of this art with everything I do. In the morning when I wake up to brush my teeth, use the restroom, and shave I think to myself, "How can I do this cheaply?" So, I came up with a routine:

I wake up in the morning, roll out of bed and turn off the fan in my room. By turning off the fan when I'm not using it, I am saving money on the electric bill. I then go and put toothpaste on my toothbrush, grab my razor and turn on the water in the shower. As the water is cleansing my body, I brush my teeth. The tube of toothpaste is used all the down to the last drop. I wrap the tube up like a coil starting at the bottom to make sure I don't waste any.

Once I complete this, I shave my stubble with a nearly empty bottle of shampoo. When my bottle of shampoo is down to its last drops, I put a couple of ounces of water in it, shake it around, and let it sit. This creates a soapy concoction that I can then use to clean up a few more times rather than wasting the remaining residue. Lastly, I relieve my bladder in the shower. This allows me to save money on the waste bill. No need to flush the toilet when you can just go in the shower!

Just like that, I knocked out four birds with one stone. I saved money by turning the fan off before I cleaned up, saved waste water by using the shower as a toilet, saved money on shaving cream because I used the same shampoo

I cleaned my hair with, and used the toothpaste all the way until the very end, all while managing to take a refreshing morning shower!

Now that we've established how to save money during the cleanup phase, let's get into the dress phase:

Next, I put on black socks, not white socks. White socks get dirtier faster than black socks do. Therefore, white socks don't last as long. I make sure to wear black ones, especially on days I know I'll be working in the yard, making mud pies with my imaginary friends, or just simply running around from place to place.

After this, I go downstairs still wearing just black socks. By running around naked, you're more aerodynamic. The more aerodynamic you are, the less energy you'll be using and thus the less food you'll need to eat. The less food you eat, the more money you'll save...Just kidding, I'm not that weird.

I put on regular clothes, then go downstairs to make sure the thermostat isn't at a money draining temperature and begin to make breakfast. Water bills can be expensive, so I clean my utensils by hand to eliminate the extra use of water from the dishwasher.

If I know I'll be going to the gym post breakfast, I always make sure to use the same pair of shorts and shirt to workout in. Depending on how sweaty and smelly you get, you can wear the same outfit two to three days in a row to eliminate the extra use of water from the washer.

When you finally do get around to washing your clothes, you can save money by air drying them rather than using the dryer. Additionally, by turning off the TV once you're done watching, the radio once you're done listening, the lights before leaving the house, and making sure the AC is at a reasonable temperature at all times throughout the day, you'll begin seeing changes in your monthly bill. These changes may be small, but they will add up!

After breakfast, I take out the trash. Instead of walking over to the side of the house with my socks on, I put on a pair of shoes. This way, I don't wear out the bottom of my socks and make holes in them. On my way to work, I make sure to take a specific route that has a gas station with the cheapest possible price per gallon. I fill up my small, fuel efficient, Toyota Camry, and head the rest of the way.

While I'm on my way, I either listen to the radio or use one of my free music apps such as Musi to listen to music. I don't use Apple Music, Spotify Premium, or SoundCloud because it costs extra money every month. Instead, I just listen to the sweet sound of saving money as my free music app plays beautiful tunes. These free music apps work just as well as the name-brand, popularized music platforms do. The only difference is the ads that pop up, which yes, are annoying, but are not $12 a month annoying!

At work, I enjoy my home-made lunch that cost me an eighth of what it cost Billy to eat his panini from Panera. Packing your own lunch allows you to get more for less. However, if I did decide to eat out, I always make sure to eat my entire plate, or take the rest home in a to-go box. I never throw away leftovers! This is like throwing away a five-dollar bill. Who would be crazy enough to do this?

On days that I have school instead of work, I make sure to take the bus (which is free to students). This saves me money on gas since I don't have to drive my car. If there was no bus or the bus cost money, then I'd buy myself a bike. If I didn't have money for a bike, I'd give cars driving by the good ole hitchhikers thumb. Sounds crazy, but I did it multiple times on my way to class after having missed the bus. There are always alternative ways to save. Get creative!

Over the course of my college tenure, I made sure to reuse my folders and binders. I used the same five folders all of college. I would purposely buy the ones that were a little more expensive, laminated, and thicker because I knew they could take a beating. Just to make sure I got my worth out of these folders; I would borrow tape from the school library and tape up the edges. This significantly increased the life span of my folders and prevented them from ripping apart. I may have only saved a total of $4 during that entire period, considering most folders are ten cents or less, but in my mind that was four meals. Four dollars is equivalent to four-dollar burgers from McDonald's. Change the way you look at your stuff—everything has a monetary value!

I wouldn't recommend taking things this far, but when I worked at a movie theater in college, I'd scrounge for pennies in seat cushions and eat leftover popcorn, candy, and hotdogs from trashcans. I didn't want to have to spend money at the food court in the mall and I never let any change go unnoticed. I was willing to do just about anything to get a free meal or find a couple extra cents. Sometimes you have to do whatever it takes.

RELATIONSHIPS

I'm a big believer that we accept the love we deserve. Frankly, that's probably one of the reasons I didn't date in college. I never found a girl who worked harder than me. Until I did, I refused to go on a second date. Discipline was attractive to me and I never found it in any girl I met. I felt like my 20's was my time to be selfish, to work hard and not have to worry about relationships and giving time to others. My time to grind, push forward and get ahead.

> *I didn't have time to think about relationships or marriage because I was already married to the money.*

If you're a lover at heart, then go ahead and love. At your own discretion. If you're going to go down this path, make sure the person you're sharing your time with isn't holding you back. Be with someone who has similar goals, works hard, and is frugal. Work to graduate debt-free together and be accountability partners. This path is not easy but there is no greater feeling than having someone you can share the same goals with.

Relationships were tough for me for a couple different reasons. I didn't have the means to pay for fancy dinners or special gifts. I used to feel like I had to steal flowers and chocolates before dates because I didn't have the money to pay for them. I still wanted to try and keep up with all the other guys who could buy their girlfriends fancy things, but there was only so much I could do.

Additionally, I couldn't help but look at relationships as distractions. I took to the Mike Tyson approach in college. Have you ever heard of it?

When Mike Tyson talks about his experience with woman while he was at the peak of his career, he says that he abstained from sex for five years. He believed it would detract from his ability to perform and detract from his ability to be the best ever. He so strongly gave the sport of boxing everything he had. He chose not to let anything, or anyone get in the way of him being the greatest boxer to ever live.

I'm sure my friends and family wondered why I didn't have a girlfriend during all of college? Why I stopped going on dates? Why I didn't go out with woman when invited? The answer was, I didn't want to lose focus. I didn't want any distractions.

What mattered most to me was graduating college debt-free and making sure my money was in the right place. I abstained from sex for months at a time, turned down girls asking to see me, chose not to go on dates, and deleted all online dating apps because they all took away from my time to work towards my goals.

I must also admit that even if I felt relationships weren't a distraction, it's hard to give your time and energy to someone else when you're constantly working. I felt it wasn't even worth getting into a relationship because of how busy I constantly was. I didn't want to hurt anyone because of the lack of attention, energy, and time that I would have been able to give. Any relationship I would have gotten into was doomed to fail.

Relationships are tough to find during college when you're trying to graduate debt-free. It's rare for a student to work three jobs, take six classes per semester, and commute from one city to the next for school. It's also rare to find someone doing the same thing. And if you are lucky enough to find someone you like doing the same thing, it's even more rare for the both of you to be able to find time to spend together.

Because of this, I just chose to ignore the idea of a relationship altogether. I stopped entertaining the thought of it ever happening and it honestly took a load of stress off my shoulders. Additionally, it allowed me to focus on my goals more intensely which benefitted my work ethic. I put the energy I would have spent in a relationship into myself and started to save more and make more than I ever had before.

If you're lucky enough to already have found a special somebody prior to getting into college, that's great. However, you won't be productive unless the other person you're dating has your back 110 percent. If your partner isn't pushing you to chase your dreams and be better every day, then you should reconsider the relationship.

When your partner isn't helping you move forward, then they're either slowing you down, or even worse, draining your positive energy. The bad thing about this is that you need every last ounce of the energy you have in order to graduate college debt-free. This journey is not easy and the energy you have is precious. If your partner is draining it, and holding you back from moving forward, then you have to let go. You can't let someone drag you down forever.

"If you're going to fall, fall forward—not backwards". – Denzel Washington

I know this may be tough to hear. I get that there is nothing better than being in love. But again, what is more important to you? You can learn to fall in love with the grind just as much as you once loved or still love your partner. You'll meet someone amazing, time and time again, but until you accomplish your goals, this person will be nothing more than a distraction. You have to stop entertaining these thoughts and reevaluate what is most important to you.

I understand this is an extreme approach to gaining an advantage and getting closer to graduating college debt-free. However, give this a try and I promise you'll be amazed with all the extra time you'll start to have. Don't talk to someone else with a relationship intent for an entire six months. No romantic outings, lustful evenings, or sexual desires fulfilled. Indulge in complete sexual abstinence.

You will find yourself to be more productive, less distracted, and extremely in tune with your goals. I hate to say that relationships get in the way of graduating college debt-free, but I sure can say that the progress I made without them, significantly outweighed the benefits of being in one.

For once, my goals got my complete and undivided attention. Relationships took second hand to this and my drive intensified. I became more in tune with what I wanted to achieve. I was able to use 100 percent of my energy on getting where I needed to go and it was incredibly effective.

I recommend everyone try this. No distractions. No interruptions. No trouble.

"The greatest invest you could ever make, is spending time on yourself". – Warren Buffet.

CHAPTER 13

WHAT ABOUT VACATIONS?

A misconception people have is that all vacations are expensive. This certainly doesn't have to be the case. You may not be going to the Bora Bora or Cabo that you were hoping for, but maybe you just need to set the bar a little lower and be a little more realistic about the destinations you choose for yourself.

Road trips are beautiful. Not only do you get the opportunity to stop at sights on the way to your destination, but you save immense amounts of money. I understand long car rides can be gruesome and flights are much easier, but the tradeoff is worth it. Road trips are a great way to bond with your friends, enjoy varying music tastes, and see the countryside.

A plane ticket to California typically goes for $450-500 depending on the airport and the time of year. Flights to New York, Chicago, and Indianapolis sit around this price as well. For anyone who knows anything about cheap travel, they know that road tripping is the way to go. Splitting the cost of gas with a few friends can cut trip costs down to $150 or less. It will take longer to get there, but it is well worth it when you are saving $250-$350 by not paying for plane tickets.

While I was in college, I took a handful of trips with my friends. I went to Colorado, North Carolina, California, Vegas, Minnesota and close to a dozen national parks. I'm sure there were people thinking, *How the hell does he have the money to do all that?* But what people don't realize is that you can travel cheaply if you do it the right way. There wasn't a single trip I took that cost me more than $500.

In Colorado, we received significant student discounts when booking our ski lodge because we talked the owner into lowering the costs. In North Carolina, we were offered a place to sleep for free in exchange for building a fence. In Minnesota, we had a free place to stay in exchange for doing landscaping; and in Arizona, we got free meals and a free room for doing the dishes in the back of a dining hall.

When traveling to Las Vegas, instead of staying in casino hotels on the Nevada side of Lake Tahoe, we stayed in little motels on the California side. We shared queen sized beds and took turns sleeping together. One night in a

Tahoe motel cost us only $36. Split between four people, we paid just $9 each.

You would think in a popular tourist town with such luxury, we would be paying hundreds of dollars a night. But this wasn't the case. I'm sure there are some parts of Lake Tahoe where this might be, but there are always other spots that have great deals. Never settle on the first place you find, be willing to do work in exchange for lower pricing, and always keep an eye out for good deals online.

ROAD TRIP CHEAPLY

Traveling is fun. It is even more fun when you do it cheaply. But how? How do you travel the country without breaking the bank? Here are four tips for you:

Number One:
First off, you need to take a fuel-efficient car. Smaller cars tend to get better gas mileage and can save you hundreds of dollars on long road trips. If there isn't enough room for bags, you can always buy a cheap roof rack to free up some space on the inside of the car. Speaking from experience, it is worth spending money on a roof rack because taking a bigger car will quickly eat up gas.

In college, I took a 4,500-mile trip in a Hyundai Elantra and it cost me the same amount as a 2,200-mile trip in a Chevy Tahoe. Gas is expensive! Don't bring a big car unless you have to!

Number Two:
Pack your own snacks! Road trips are fun but there are definitely times when it gets boring. When we get bored on a road trip, there are typically three things we tend to do: 1) play on our phones, 2) sleep and 3) eat.

So, what do we do?

We pull over to the next gas station we see, run inside, and grab sour gummy worms, beef jerky, Cheetos, Snickers bar, Doritos, a Snapple, and a Gatorade. Pretty accurate? I know I've done this a few times myself. But, these quick stops add up. By the end of the trip you can very easily rack up close to $100 worth of snacks. Instead of doing this, bring your own snacks and save your money!

Number Three:

Stay at campsites or in cheap motels. I've never been to a campsite that was more expensive than $25 a night. Similarly, I've never stayed at a motel that was more expensive than $45 a night. When you divide these prices by three to five people, the total cost for a night stay is no more than $15 a person. These prices are hard to beat compared to the $100-$300 nightly prices at nice hotels or luxurious resorts.

Both places get you the same thing: a roof over your head and a place to sleep. When trying to save money, there are always reasonable options. You just need to keep your eyes open!

For example, when I went to Zion National Park and Yosemite National Park, all the campsites were completely full. Stupidly, we didn't reserve our campsite ahead of time. We frantically tried to find a place to set up our tent before nightfall. In an act of desperation, we pulled up to a campsite closest to us and asked random people if they wouldn't mind us putting our tents up next to them. To our surprise, nobody turned us down.

The other campers were more than happy to allow us to share their space with them as they knew we were young college students trying to save our money. The other campers were just happy to see us expressing our love for adventure. I wouldn't depend on this happening every time you go camping, but I can say it has worked for my friends and I on multiple occasions. It is worth a try!

Number Four:

When traveling overseas, hostels are a great place to stay at a fair price. Hostels are also a great place to meet other people traveling cheaply, which in return is beneficial because you can get tips and advice on ways to save money as you travel in the country you're visiting.

The downside of traveling overseas is the cost of plane tickets. However, there are a few ways around this. The easiest way to get guaranteed tickets at a lower price is to buy your tickets months in advance. The earlier you buy your plane tickets, the cheaper they will be.

If you want to go a step further, you can. By purchasing tickets with layovers and gaps in between the connecting flights, you can save even more. I recently went to Ireland with my sister and we slept in the airport overnight so that we didn't have to pay extra for a connecting flight with no layover in between. A trip that could have taken just eleven hours, ended up taking thirty-six hours. It was brutal, but we saved a couple hundred bucks and that was worth it to us!

7 QUICK TIPS

1) Need an extra blanket and headphones? After taking a flight, keep the blanket and headphones they give you.

2) If one of your friends is hesitant on taking their car for the road trip, offer to pay for their share of gas. This is a great way to incentivize agreement since it saves them money.

3) When going on road trips, never take your own car. The wear and tear will hurt later down the line. Instead, take a friend's car and follow the above tip. If this doesn't work, take a greyhound. Greyhounds offer cross country bus rides for a small fee.

4) If you do fly, just make sure you pay for basic economy. First class is not worth the increase in price.

5) Don't speed. Faster driving requires more fuel to get you the same distance.

6) If you want to travel but need money fast, you can fundraise online. Money raising platforms such as Go-Fund-Me can get you quick money from family and friends.

7) When you plan correctly, extravagant trips will no longer seem out of reach. Give it a try!

HEAT WAVE, I NEED TO BE SAVED

I went to the Austrian Alps with my family when I was fifteen. During that week, Europe experienced one of the worst heat waves in its history. This same week, the AC broke in the car my family took. Timely, I know!

Five of us crammed into a Prius sized car, with temperatures hitting 35 degrees Celsius during the day (92 degrees Fahrenheit). The car would get so hot during the middle of the day that my brother and I would literally sit in our underwear. As sweat dripped off our steaming hair and touching arms, we did everything we could to cool ourselves off. We poured water on our heads, created makeshift paper fans, and even took turns blowing cool air onto each other's faces. We did this just about all day every day for six days straight.

My mom refused to get the AC fixed because she didn't want to pay for it. It would have made the trip a lot more pleasurable, but it was expensive, so I understood. Saving money on road trips isn't always pretty, but it does call for a funny story!

"Sometimes you need to experience the bad in order to enjoy the good." – Leon Brown

DAYTONA 500 MAY COST YOU $500

When you're on a highway that looks like there will never be an end, it's easy to let your mind wander. When you space out like this it's easy to forget about the speed limit. This is why you should always use cruise control. If you don't, you may end up speeding and making the same mistake I did.

In college, I was on a road trip through Arizona, Nevada, and California. My friends and I visited three national parks, Lake Tahoe, and Las Vegas. The trip had gone perfectly. Free campsites, cheap hotels, and friends' couches to crash on during the trip up and back.

We got into the national parks for free because it was the 103rd birthday week of national parks in the U.S. Our dollar general grocery runs and home-made meals kept things cheap. We even got out of a speeding ticket on the way up with a little smile and a wave.

The trip was affordable, the Sierra Nevada mountain range was unlike anything we had ever seen before, and the weather was gorgeous. Eight days later, it was time to leave. The rest of us dropped our buddy Dylan off at the airport around 10:30am, grabbed lunch at 11am, and started our trek to Tucson, Arizona at 12pm.

Our plan was to drive thirteen hours from Reno, Nevada to Tucson, Arizona stopping only for gas, food, and to use the restroom. We figured we would make it to Tucson, Arizona around 2am. Not terrible, but we forgot one thing—time zones.

The one-hour time difference actually had us looking at a 3am arrival time. This may not seem terrible, but you don't know what it's like until you've spent the past eight days hiking mountains, traveling across the country and a questionable amount of REM sleep to account for. I mean come on—we were in Vegas.

With that said, we figured going a little over the speed limit to make up some time wouldn't hurt. The five-over rule turned into fifteen-over, which turned into thirty-over…and I'll just stop there for the sake of my mother reading this. We were making great time, shaved off twenty minutes of the trip in just a matter of three hours. Twelve hours later that number could have been easily been over an hour, putting us right at our initial planned arrival time of 2am.

Speeding down the two-lane 95-N, with nothing but mountains and cactus all around us was exhilarating. Until we saw the red and blue lights flashing behind us. We knew it. I knew it. No getting out of this one.

Esmeralda County has more traffic facilities than any other place in the country, the cop lectured. He then went back to his car, took what felt like forever, and came back to give me the largest ticket I had ever seen: $435 and a whole lot of regretful thinking to carry with me the rest of the way home.

To make matters worse, the traffic stop took more than twenty-five minutes. This meant all that time we spent speeding to make up for the change in time zone, ended up being for nothing. No time made up and $435 in the hole. Ouch!

Lessons to be learned:

1) Sometimes doing things faster than you're supposed to results in a worse outcome.

2) Cruise control is your best friend on road trips. Flip that sucker on and let the car do her thing.

3) Don't get carried away. It's easy to get caught up in the nothingness around you when driving on open roads. Remember that there are still rules—including a speed limit. Don't let the monotonous surroundings trick you. Take my word for it! It was an expensive lesson; $640 in total, five hours of Texas driving school, and five hours of Nevada driving school. It was not fun!

CHAPTER 14

BUDGETING

Budgeting is one of the most important aspects to saving money and graduating college debt-free. It is important to set goals for yourself so that you can see when you're starting to veer off path. Budgeting will help keep you accountable so that you're never overspending. The more strictly you follow your budget, the more money you'll save and the closer you'll get to graduating debt-free.

It is hard to say exactly how much you should budget each month since we all live in different cities, have different jobs, different costs of living, and varying tuition costs. However, this template below can be used and followed to help give you a start. Also, I'll give a real-world example so you can get an idea of how I budgeted myself.

With that said, there is no right or wrong way to budget if you're saving money and getting closer to your financial goals. Your budget does not have to look like this. It can be much more detailed or just a couple numbers written down on a McDonalds napkin—as long as it works. Of course, the more specific you are, the better results you will get. But the point is, this isn't a beauty contest. Do what works for you and follow it as closely as possible. Stay discipline and you will see awesome results.

YOUR BUDGET LIST

Thanks to seedime.com[4] and nyfamily-digital.com[5] for the categories and budget template list below. Not all these sections will apply to you. If this is the case, just leave the box blank. However, on the rest of the template, fill out your average monthly, quarterly, six month, and annual numbers. Then calculate your monthly expenses and subtract that from your monthly income to see where you fall. This will give you a good idea as to what you can cut out of list of expenses to help you save more money. Follow this budget tightly, work extra jobs to make more money and you'll be on your way to graduating college debt-free!

---

[4] https://seedtime.com/basic-personal-budget-categories/
[5] nyfamily-digital.com

Food Section: Groceries, Restaurants, Pet Food/Treats

Housing Section: Mortgage, Rent, Property Taxes, Household Repairs, HOA Dues

Utilities Section: Electricity, Water, Heating, Garbage, Phone Bill, Cable, Internet

Transportation Section: Fuel, Tires, Oil Changes, Maintenance, Parking Fees, Repairs, DMV Fees, Vehicle Replacement

Medical Section: Primary Care, Dental Care, Specialty Care (Orthodontics, Optometrists), Medications, Medical Devices

Clothing Section: For Work, School, Weddings, Season

Household Items: Toiletries, Laundry Detergent, Dishwasher Detergent, Cleaning Supplies, Tools

Education: Tuition, School Supplies, Books, Tutoring, Conferences

Savings: Emergency Fund, Money Set Aside

Gifts: Birthday, Anniversary, Wedding, Christmas, Special Occasion

Fun Money: Entertainment, Games, Eating Out, Spontaneous Giving, Vacations, Subscriptions—Such as Netflix.

Retirement: Financial Planning, Investing, 401k

Personal: Gym Memberships, Hair Cuts, Salon Services, Cosmetics, Babysitter, Child Support, Alimony, Subscriptions

Insurance: Health Insurance, Homeowner's Insurance, Renter's Insurance, Auto Insurance, Life Insurance, Disability Insurance, Identity Theft Protection, Long term Care Insurance

BUDGET EXAMPLE

Budget Worksheet for College Students

INCOME:	Daily	Monthly	Semesterly	Yearly
From Jobs (after taxes)				
From Parents / Family				
From Financial Aid				
Miscellaneous Income				
Other				
Total Income:	0	0	0	0

FIXED EXPENSES:	Daily	Monthly	Semesterly	Yearly
Rent / Housing				
Food / Meal Plan				
Car Payment				
Car Insurance & Registration				
Tuition & Fees				
Loan / Credit Card Payments				
Telephone / Cell Phone				
Utilities				
Other				
Total Fixed Expenses:	0	0	0	0

FLEXIBLE EXPENSES:	Daily	Monthly	Semesterly	Yearly
Eating Out				
Clothing				
Books				
Entertainment				
Public Transportation				
Cable				
Internet Access				

For me, budgeting has always been fun. Tracking my receipts and looking back at my expenses for each month, quarter, or year has always been extremely eye opening. It always surprises me how much I can spend without realizing it. These monthly and quarterly reviews are so important. They will help you reflect on your spending habits so that you can readjust accordingly.

It's easy to get off course when you're having fun. It's easy to go watch a movie with your significant other, go out to eat with friends, or go to the arcade with your family. The money comes slow but goes fast. Make sure you check on your budget often. The more you check your progress, the more success you'll have with following your budget, and the more you'll save.

CHALLENGE: Create a budget and start following it closely. After a few months of tracking your expenses, review your progress. In a social media post, share how much you've managed to save by cutting out your bad spending habits. Make sure to include the hashtags #gettingahead and #ultraproductive.

RECEIPT BOY

To help me better budget, I kept all my receipts for an entire year during college. These receipts included big things like rent, utilities, and car insurance, all the way down to simply paying a parking meter or buying sunflower seeds at the gas station. I kept every single one. At the end of the year, there were roughly 650 receipts in total. This means I purchased nearly two things every day…Ridiculous!

When totaling my year of expenses, I realized how much I had fooled myself. I fooled myself into believing that I was a master budgeter. I tricked myself into believing that going out to eat once or twice a week was okay. I tricked myself into believing that it was okay to buy a new shirt since everyone else had one. I tricked myself into believing it was okay to go to an NBA playoff game, even though the tickets were extremely expensive. Upon totaling my receipts and looking at my numbers for the year, I had spent a whopping $34,000.

I quickly realized that I wasn't being as frugal as I had once believed. I was spending way more than I had initially thought. I was trying to keep up with my friends, when I truly didn't have the means to do so. This made me realize the importance of budgeting, living at home, and always living below my means. I learned that as much as you make will be as much as you spend, if you try and keep up with the Joneses.

My receipts for the entire year:

HOW DID I BUDGET IN COLLEGE?

Despite spending $34,000 in that one year, I budgeted as hard as I could. Apparently, I wasn't doing as good of a job as I had believed. I do know, however, that there were some things that I did well. Here is an unorganized account of what I did to budget and what you can do to save as well:

When I was in college, I never let food go bad. One time I had sausage in my freezer that was over a month and a half old. All my roommates told me to throw it out because it would make me sick. Before any of them could do it for me, the sausage was on the grill cooking. I ate it. It was delicious. Old yellow broccoli was my next adventure. Unlike the sausage, the broccoli did not taste too good.

Expired this, expired that—I ate everything because I hated wasting money. I'm a big believer in eating what you have at home before going out and buying more food. There should never be an excuse to throw food out. I ate until my pantry was dry. If I bought it, I ate it.

There was a period where I ate canned chicken and ramen noodles for two weeks straight because I didn't want to waste any of it. I didn't want to have to toss out ten cent ramen packs. This ladies and gentlemen is the art of frugality on full display.

When it came to mainstream clothing and trying to fit in, I'd always find ways to buy cheaply. Chinese e-commerce companies such as AliExpress and Alibaba were goldmines. I could purchase jerseys, shoes, and watches all for a quarter of the price that they were being sold for in the U.S. This allowed me to stay in style without breaking my bank.

Phone chargers, phone cases, and Bluetooth headphones from AliExpress and Alibaba were always a must buy as well. The quality was never as good, but they kept me from having to spend ridiculous amounts of money on items that would probably go out of style just as quickly as they had been introduced.

When taking graduation photos, I used an iPhone. Afterwards, I downloaded a free app to edit the pictures myself to improve their quality. iPhone cameras take pictures nearly as well as professional cameras. No need to pay hundreds of dollars for an expensive camera or photographer.

Many schools also have career service centers that have professional photographers that will take your pictures free of charge! The schools pay for it so take advantage of these amazing opportunity. Some schools even have career closets where students can rent suits and professional attire for free. The only thing you pay for is the dry cleaning after you use it—never costing more than $10.

When grocery shopping, I'd always pay for generic items. I never bought name brand items as they were always too expensive! No Fruit Loops, Captain Crunch, or Cinnamon Toast Crunch. It was always Far Out Fruities, Crisp Berry Crunch, and Cinnamon Swirls.

When choosing a grocery store, always look for wholesale clubs. Sam's club and HEB should always be picked over Randall's and corner stores. There is no significant difference in quality, but a huge difference in price. I know what I'd choose if I was trying to graduate from college debt-free.

Aside from shopping for clothes and groceries, there are other ways you can save money too. For example, when taking classes, you should always make sure to sit next to students that are attentive, respectful, and care about what the teacher is saying. These students, who stay off their phones and enjoy learning, are the kids you want to sit by and work on projects with. Your group mates will directly reflect your overall grade in the class. Good grades mean passing classes, which means saving money. It also means a higher GPA which may translate to better jobs once you graduate.

HIGH SCHOOL BUDGET

During my high school years, my budgeting was just as insane—if not more insane than it was in college. During homecoming, I took my date to Schlotzsky's. When it was time to order, I made her order a small sandwich instead of a large because it was too expensive. Looking back, I can imagine how bad that looked on my part. However, at the time, that extra $4 was a big deal to me.

As a fast growing, hungry kid, it was hard to budget on food in high school. Yet, if I hadn't, I would have easily spent hundreds of dollars every semester. Instead, I made peanut butter jelly sandwiches every morning before I went to school. These home packed lunches helped me save like a Dave Ramsey foot soldier.

PB&J's every lunch time got old quick, but I knew an older version of myself would appreciate my discipline. Any time I ran out of PB&J's and needed something quick to eat, I'd send it to the dollar menu. McDonalds, Wendy's, Whataburger, Sonic, thank you for helping me save money...and for the muffin top. My future bank account thanked me but not my future treadmill sessions.

Eating out is convenient. There is no doubt about that. You don't have to spend time buying groceries, prepping the food, or cleaning the dishes. The food is cheap, the service is quick, and you leave on a full stomach. I mean, it is called "fast-food" for a reason.

But what if these quick meals become normal and routine? What would that mean for us? What if this routine became a habit? Not just for breakfast, but for lunch, and dinner too?

Let's look at this in-depth. Here is a scenario: You want to get away from the workplace for lunch, so you head down the road to Arby's. Or you want to grab something to eat on the way home from work to make traffic a little more bearable, so you stop by Whataburger. Tasty, delicious, and convenient. Yet, expensive!

Expensive? Yes. Not initially, but these little stops add up. You may be thinking, "do people actually do this?" The answer is yes, they do. There are people who eat out for every meal of the day. If this is you, it is time to change this routine. But how did we get here?

As inflation continues to rise and the cost of living increases, Americans now must work longer hours to support themselves. And with more hours working, Americans now have less time to stop at the grocery store and less time to prep their own meals.

However, busy is an excuse. It is just a matter of not having your priorities straight. If you want to graduate college debt-free, you will make saving money your top priority. Every dollar saved is a dollar made. Every meal prepped is a plus to your bank account. Every fast-food chain passed on is a win in the books.

You can't graduate college debt-free if you aren't budgeting appropriately. If you are a restaurant rat, you need to reconsider your habits. You can either spend less than $2 on a loaf of bread and under $8 on jars of peanut butter and jelly, or you can spend $10 on one meal at a restaurant or fast-food joint.

The meal lasts you one sitting, whereas the loaf of bread and the PB&J makes you twelve sandwiches for multiple sittings. You can even throw in a banana, bag of chips, trail mix, and a protein bar, and it would still be cheaper than a fast-food meal.

When you really sit down, crunch the numbers, and think about it, eating out isn't the smartest use of your money. So, make your own damn lunch!

PEANUT BUTTER JELLY TIME

I ate peanut butter jelly sandwiches every day for eight years. During high school and college, I brought my own lunch to school, work, and sometimes even to parties. Unfortunately, I was growing so much that my appetite outgrew eating one sandwich alone. So, what did I do? Eat at fast food restaurants to fill the void? Rarely, instead, I just started eating two peanut butter jelly sandwiches at lunch instead of one.

Any time I left the house, I would pack a lunch. During those four years I saved easily over $6,000 by making my own lunch/meals every day.

My brother spent $3,000 on fast food in a six-month period while he was in high school. He ate out nearly every single day. This just goes to show how quickly eating out can rack up. It only took my brother sixth months to blow through what he made in an entire year working at Chipotle.

With this said, make your own damn lunch. Don't be like my brother in high school. Home cook your meals, buy your own groceries, and save your money! Your bank account will thank you at the end of the month!

THE EXPERT LAW: 10,000 HOURS

In Malcom Gladwell's book, Outliers, he says you become an expert once you spend 10,000 hours working towards something. I put in my 10,000 hours, making peanut butter jelly sandwiches.

My PB&J's are of the highest quality. They have an unparalleled peanut butter to jelly ratio, the perfect spread-to-edge coverage, and a hint of love that will make you itch for more. I am the master peanut butter jelly chef. Any of my friends will vouch for me. If you ever see me in public, invite me over to make you a peanut butter jelly sandwich. You won't be disappointed.

CHALLENGE: Make your own lunch and post a picture on social media with the hashtags #gettingahead and #ultraproductive.

SOME WILL NEVER UNDERSTAND, BUT THAT'S OKAY

I used to listen to a song by Mick Jenkins called "Value Village". His chorus, "Don't listen, save money," helped me budget during my high school and college years. Anytime I wanted to buy something I didn't need or buy a meal that was outside of my budget, I'd be reminded to save the money instead. I could relate to the song so much that over time it became my own personal theme song. It was comforting knowing someone else out there was living the same way I was.

I remember going on a date one time after listening to Value Village and I was telling my date how my phone screen had cracked. I explained to her that I ordered parts for a new screen online, from a company in China, to save a little money. My plan was to put the screen back on myself, then sell my phone for what it would have been originally worth. My date never understood why I was going through all this hassle just to repair a screen. "It won't cost you more than $100 to have it fixed at the mall," she said.

She did have a point, but what she didn't realize is that for me, $100 was a lot of money. That $100 helped me pay for my monthly grocery bill, my phone bill, or a few tanks of gas.

This whole experience made me realize that some people truly don't know the value of a dollar. Despite, being embarrassed, I still felt like I won. By using my sister's hairdryer, I melted the adhesive on the screen so that I could pop it off and put on the new screen that I had bought from China. The new screen and the parts cost me eight dollars. When sold, I made $100 more than the phone would have gone for with a cracked screen. My total profit was $92. And as I got back into my car after selling the phone, I plugged my iPod into the AUX cord, and listened to the sweet tune of Value Village as I drove off.

"Don't listen, save money... Don't listen save money"

THE PLANET FITNESS MINDSET

Working out is great. Not only does it help slim down that beer belly of yours, but it also floods your brain with endorphins. You know, the feel-good juices our brain produces. I hear people say all too often that gym memberships are too expensive. I disagree. Gym memberships are expensive if you let them be expensive. You have a large selection of gyms to choose from. LifeTime Fitness memberships can be up to $150 dollars a month, Golds gym $90, LA

Fitness $50. On the other hand, you have Crunch Fitness and Planet Fitness which only charge $10 a month. In this case, less is more.

I often laugh when I hear my friends say they're broke when I know they go to LifeTime Fitness. I know damn well this problem of theirs could be fixed if they stopped going to LifeTime Fitness and instead transitioned to the good ol' judgment free zone of Planet Fitness.

I understand the equipment may not be up to the standard that some people like or that the rules may be a little ridiculous, but at the end of the day you're saving nearly $800 dollars a year. And in all honestly, are you really playing racquetball, taking Zumba classes, and using the slides at the LifeTime pool enough to justify the extra $80 a month?

Planet Fitness is just $10 a month for a white card. If you are feeling lavish, you can even pay an extra $10 a month to get the black card. This black card allows you to use the tanning beds and bring in a free guest with no limit on the amount of times this privilege is exercised. No other gym allows free guests, especially none for the price that Planet Fitness offers.

As long as you don't have any scream lifting tendencies or the constant urge to judge others harshly, then you won't have to worry about the lunk alarm being pulled or breaking the rules of the judgement free zone. Ultimately, Planet Fitness is a great way to stay within the confines of your budget, while still getting to exercise at a quality gym.

What if you just absolutely can't do Planet Fitness and still can't afford the gym you want to go to? Then work there one or two days a week and get a free membership. It's simple. There's always a solution to every problem. Don't make it harder than it needs to be. Keep it simple and figure it out.

SAVE THAT MONEY

Some of these budgeting methods and tactics are easy to mimic yourself. Yet so many of you will choose not to listen and it will cost you in the long run. So, why do you do it even though you know you shouldn't? Bad habits.

Begin working on saving money every single day. The more you practice saving and saying no to unnecessary expenditures, the more this mindset of frugality will become a habit. Consistency is key. This will be the beginning of a new you. Saving a couple dollars every day will turn into massive savings over time. You'll be able to graduate college debt-free and set yourself up for future success.

CHALLENGE: Call your bank today and create automatic withdrawals. Every month have the bank withdraw $25-$100 from your main spending account into an untouchable account that can only be used on educational expenses such as tuition, books, and school supplies. This may sound like a small feat but watch as this account balance grows exponentially over time—helping you pay off your college expenses faster! After you call your bank, share your experience online. Use the hashtags #gettingahead and #ultraproductive.

CHAPTER 15

WATCH THE MOVIE MINIMALISM

Minimalism is the idea of living with less. Minimizing the things you buy and do, so that you can put your energy and resources toward something more rewarding. By getting rid of the things you no longer use and eliminating all the cluster that makes your life overwhelming, you will be freed from self.

Abundance is not always a good thing. Often, having too much going on at once or having too much stuff is more of a hassle than it is good. Everything must be done and had in moderation to maintain sanity. To find this peace within, you need to reorganize your external world. You can do this by adopting a lifestyle of minimums.

The responsibilities you have are not as important as you think, the material possessions you buy are not as fulfilling as you thought and the people you're trying to impress don't care nearly as much as you believe.

By reorganizing your focus onto what's truly important, you will always be spending time on the things that make you happiest. Money will be spent on necessities rather than wants and your relationships will flourish.

We as human beings have limited energy. Therefore, we must be extremely intentional with what we spend our time doing and thinking. Remove all the negativity and watch as the *excess* transforms into *access* to a happier life.

This concept can be translated to all facets of life. Let's first determine where you're currently at.

> *"Minimalism is the concept of reducing the number of material possessions one has to create a sense of freedom from self. We tend to give too much meaning to our things, often forsaking our health, our relationships, our passions, our personal growth, and our desire to contribute beyond ourselves."* – The Minimalists

The Minimalist Assessment

Answer these questions:

CLOTHES

- How many shirts in your closet have you NOT worn in the past month?

- How many purchases of the clothes in your closet were spontaneous? i.e. You thought you looked good in the changing room mirror and after that you never wore it again.

- Have you noticed a pattern in your outfits? i.e. Wearing the same two or three different shirts to the gym every week, the same two or three shorts with friends or the same two or three shoes at school.

- Do you have dresses that you rarely wear?

- Do you have shoes that collect dust?

- Does it ever bother you that you have extra clothes?

Clothes are clutter. Imagine not having to worry about what outfit you'll wear because you only have one or two to choose from. There's no point in having dozens of shirts, pants, and shoes if you never wear them.

FRIENDS

- Do you have friends that are constantly negative?

- Do you have friends that are stagnant in life, not getting better, or even worse, regressing?

- Do you spend time with people that get on your nerves or don't support your goals?

- Do you spend your time and energy trying to please others but get nothing in return?

- Do you hang around people that spend more than they save?

- Do you spend time with people that don't understand the value of the dollar?

- Do you hang around people that are less intelligent than you are?

- Do you spend time with people that don't respect hard work and ambition?

- Are your goals and aspirations much larger than the people you spend the most time with?

If the answer to any of these questions is yes, then you need to consider removing these people from your life. Don't let the negativity of others drain you. This stuff is infectious, and it will bring you down to their level. Break away from people like this, cut ties, and watch as your life begins to improve.

DECISIONS

- Is this decision going to help or hurt me?

- Does this decision align with my long-term goals?

- What does my past experience tell me about this?

- How does this decision fit in with my needs?

- Does this decision fulfill my essential principles or priorities?

- Am I making this decision from an emotional state?

- Do I understand the consequences of my decision for myself as I can reasonably predict them?

Your decisions are the driving force behind your subsequent success or failure. Every choice you make is either pushing you forward or pulling you back. Make sure your resolve is intentional and purpose driven. Don't lose track of the end goal.

INTROSPECTION

Continue to reassess your external world. If it doesn't align with your internal ambition, then it's time to reorganize again. To minimize the energy draining aspects of life, ask yourself these simple questions:

- Do I need this? Will this make me happier?

- Is this a mutually beneficial relationship? Does this person push me to become a better version of myself daily?

- Does this decision align with my goals, values, and desires? Am I choosing this from a logical perspective or an emotional one?

Ironically, minimalism will help you maximize your life. It is the quickest path to fulfillment and gratitude. Remove the EXCESS and welcome the AC-CESS. Give it a try!

"Minimalism isn't about living with nothing—it's about living with less. Stripping your possessions back to what genuinely adds value to your life, makes you happy, and helps you function. When you dampen the noise around the things you love, they become so much more exciting." – Joshua Fields Millburn & Ryan Nicodemus

CHALLENGE: Do a deep clean and get rid of all the clothes you don't need. When you've sorted all your items, throw them into a box, and post a picture on social media with the hashtags #gettingahead and #ultraproductive.

WATCH WHAT YOU SPEND

Broke has become normal. Seventy percent of Americans are living paycheck to paycheck. Yet, ninety percent of the population avoids living a minimalist lifestyle. Instead, they buy TV sets, fancy bottled water, and designer makeup, while only ten percent of the population buys business books, goal planners, and vision boards. There's no secret to getting ahead. It's all hard work, saving, and investing your time into the right things.

Two of the most valuable things you can learn at a young age is the value of a dollar and that how hard you work translates to the level of success you'll have. Effort always precedes natural ability.

For some people, making money doesn't come easy. Every dollar earned is an accomplishment. Yet, the accomplishment is only realized if the money earned is spent properly.

We all know people who seem to always be broke. It's a shame. Not because they don't have any money to spend but because they're spending the little money they do have on the wrong things.

The sad reality of this is that a lot of these people always seem to have the newest shoes, phone, bracelets, watches, etc. They're always the ones who go out and eat four times a week and are members of expensive gyms. They're the ones with the nicest cars, buy everyone drinks at the bar, and go on luxurious vacations.

But why? After closely studying the people around me, here is my hypothesis as to why people spend carelessly. I call it the Spender 1, 2, and 3-character flaws. Let's look at these varying character flaws for high school and college students.

Spender 1: The Bandwagon

This person always wants to keep up with the Joneses and can't handle the blow to the ego if they're not continuously the center of attention. They always have to keep up with the crowd. They get the newest phone, watch the most popular shows, and hop on all the latest trends.

Spender 2: The Yes Man

This person doesn't have the mental toughness to turn people down. They always want to have fun, spend time around others, and enjoy the finer things in life. Anytime they are invited to go out, they say yes. They hate letting others down.

Spender 3: The Dependent

This person has never had to work a day in their life. Their parents are enablers. They get an allowance every two weeks; they are constantly calling their mom and dad to transfer money into their bank account, and they refuse to work—trust fund babies.

Spenders 1, 2, and 3 all have serious problems. If these habits aren't addressed and fixed early on, then the rest of their lives will be terribly affected. If any of these spenders are you, act now. By doing so, you might still be savable.

SPENDER 1 – The Bandwagon

If you fall under Spender 1, you can, and will change. It will take time and practice, but you can do it. Personally, I can say I've been one to crave attention nearly all my life. It feels good to be wanted. It feels good when other people are interested in you. It feels good when your voice gets heard. However, getting attention through materialistic things and going along with the crowd means nothing. And if you stand for nothing, you'll fall for anything.

With this said, there is no need to try and be someone you're not. Impressing others and always putting on a show is exhausting. You don't have to be perfect all the time. We're human. No money spent can make up for your flaws in character, so just be yourself. I promise that's enough. Live below your means and surround yourself with people who accept you, not for the things you have, but the love you offer.

"Do not spoil what you have by desiring what you have not." – Ann Brashers

SPENDER 2 – The Yes Man

If you fall under Spender 2, you can, and you will change. But first you need to stop caring so much about what other people think. Forget what other people say about you. You can't please everyone.

Other people's judgment never helped you. Did their judgement help you get up this morning? Did their opinions help you on your test? Did their criticism help you get that extra job? No, definitely not.

Then why care so much about what others say? It is pointless.

"Don't lose sleep over the opinions of sheep." – John G. Stevens

When I was in college, people would say, "There couldn't be a worse time to stop drinking! That would have definitely made college harder!" But here is how I looked at it: There couldn't have possibly been a better time to stop drinking.

This made college easier. I had my priorities in order and was focused on the right things. My energy was 100 percent on making money and getting good grades. Because of this, I was able to get ahead. There couldn't possibly have been a better time.

Yes, I sacrificed my social life and put plenty of relationships on the back burner, but I was so passionate about graduating debt-free that it was worth it. I wasn't trying to be antisocial; I was just trying to protect myself. I knew what I had to do to get what I wanted, and I wasn't going to let anything get in the way of that.

What are you sacrificing to get what you want?

If your future is important enough to you, then learn to say no. If you're genuinely serious about graduating college debt-free, then forget anything and everything that gets in your way. Stay focused, be intentional, and ignore the distractions.

The opinions of others don't shape you. The only person who decides who you are and who you're going to be is you. The only opinion that matters is your own. Run your own race and learn to say no to all the negative influences. The more no's you say, the more yes's you'll get—think about it.

SPENDER 3 – The Dependent

If you fall under Spender 3, you can, and you will change. However, this is going to be an extra difficult path for you. Spender 3 is the person who doesn't have to work for what they have. These are the people who get an allowance from their parents every two weeks and are constantly calling their mom and dad any time their card is declined so that money can be put into their bank account.

If this is or has been you up to this point, I'm happy for you. Make sure to show appreciation and gratitude towards your parents often. However, your parents were enablers your whole life, which makes you dependent, and this is a tough spot to be in.

Dependents don't know how to work hard. I'm sure there are a few exceptions in this group, but I truly have yet to meet a dependent who is a grinder—not in the library, but in life. There is a difference between someone who is studious in school and someone who displays diligence outside of the classroom.

Wisdom over intellect, that is the true mark of a leader. If you're able bodied and level minded, but still dependent on others, it is time to change. There is nothing worse than someone who thinks they deserve success without having to work for it. It doesn't work like that.

Life doesn't give handouts. You can't expect anything. There are no guarantees. If you want something, you have to go out and get it on your own.

Go get a job and begin learning the value of a dollar. If you don't, you're slowly getting behind. As others are learning to live their lives independently, you're still having your hand held. And when times get tough and there is nobody around to take care of you, you're going to fall apart. Don't be dependent on others and don't let anyone be your enabler. Instead, be the creator of your own destiny.

"Don't invite broke into your life." – Unknown

CHAPTER 16

TAKE CARE OF YOUR THINGS

It is extremely important to act as if everything you own is irreplaceable. How would you treat the things you own, if someone told you right now, that you won't be able to buy anything new for the rest of your life?

You have to re-wear the same clothes, run in the same shoes, use the same pots and pans, drive the same car, work on the same laptop, etc. If this were the case, I'm sure you'd start treating these items differently.

If you had to wear the same shoes for the rest of your life, you'd think twice about taking shortcuts through the mud. You'd probably also check your car fluids regularly, make sure not to cut meat in your pans to prevent scratching the bottoms, and wear a napkin over your lap when eating spaghetti. Hell, maybe you'd even eat at your house naked, so you don't get stains on your clothes.

Every time I went to the gym, I would wear the same one or two old shirts, one or two old shorts and the same pair of athletic shoes. When those shirts got sweaty, wrinkly, and pitted out. When they got holes, stains and stretched. I wouldn't be upset. Why? Because this is what I had planned for.

I set aside a few garments specifically for athletic activity so that my nicer clothes wouldn't get wore out. I made sure that each of the clothes in my wardrobe was assigned a specific purpose. A specific label, for a specific use. A few winter items, a few for summer. A few to workout in, a few for professional environments. A few for dates, a few for hanging out around the house. And all taken care of with delicacy and care.

This mindset allowed me to extend the life of my clothing and also had a multitude of other benefits that can help you too. By arranging your clothes in an orderly fashion, you can keep tabs on your things. By putting them back in the same place after every use, you can quickly find when something is missing or has been misplaced.

For example, my junior year of college, a friend of mine borrowed a belt unannounced. I noticed it was gone the same day it had been taken. I was so on top of keeping an eye on my things that when my belt went missing, I caught it immediately.

I then went on a weeklong hunt to find my belt. I called all my friends and texted all my roommates. They knew if the belt wasn't returned to me by the end of the week, someone was getting their butt kicked.

By the end of the week the belt was returned to me. Not just to my room, but to the exact same spot in the closet it had been hanging earlier that week. It was a close call but my friends learned their lesson.

That same winter break, I went to Breckenridge, Colorado on a ski trip with friends. After a long day of major wipeouts and minor concussions, I hopped in the shower to clean up. After my much-needed shower, I walked over to my suitcase to put on my outfit—my favorite pair of black joggers and a boxing hoodie. There was just one problem.

The joggers weren't anywhere to be found.

Infuriated, I interrogated everyone in that cabin. Looking back, this was probably not the best way to handle the situation. I had wrongly assumed that someone in the cabin had taken the pants out of my suitcase with malicious intent. I am still quite embarrassed for letting my fuse blow. However, in my defense, it took over an hour of searching until they finally turned up.

I finally found my pants underneath a pile of dirty clothes and all was forgiven. Apparently, I had left the pants out the night before and they had gotten mixed up.

When dealing with your things, you need to run a tight ship and keep tabs on your items at all times. This also goes for around your apartment, house, car, condo, and place of work. When something does get misplaced, don't just shrug it off. Instead, treat everything like you'll never have a chance to get a new one. By doing this, you will never have to replace your personal belongings.

Taking care of your things means they last longer. If they last longer, that means you don't need to buy new ones. If you don't have to buy new ones, then you save money. When you save money, you realize that taking care of your things is worthwhile. When you realize this, it makes it easier for it to become a habit. And when it comes a habit, you begin to realize the benefit. With realization comes acceptance and with acceptance comes transformation. And that is a win.

"Don't be careless with your money." – Dave Ramsey

THE BEST PIECE OF ADVICE I EVER RECEIVED

The best piece of advice I ever received was from a young guy who I initially thought was a jerk. Upon reflection, his simple two-word answer to my question about life advice was not out of apathy, but rather sincerity. These two words repeatedly proved to be the most important piece of advice that I would ever receive in my life. What was the two-word phrase? Common Sense.

Common sense is a simple yet very important philosophy to live by. It is so simple that it is usually overlooked. However, it can change your entire perspective on life, as it did mine. Let me give you an example scenario:

A young college student just bought a brand-new iPhone 11. While this student is at the checkout line purchasing the iPhone, the employee running the counter asks if the student would like to purchase a case for the phone at a twenty percent discount. The student politely says no and carries on with her day.

The student is so excited to have her new phone that she runs out of the store. She drives to her next class, sits in on the lecture, and then heads home immediately after.

As she walks to her car after class, she pulls the new phone out of her pocket. She doesn't have a good grip on the phone, and it slips right out of her hand.

The phone falls and hits the pavement in the blink of an eye. Screen shattered, home button broken, front camera cracked.

Just a few hours earlier she could have bought a case for her phone. Instead, she chose not to. Whose fault is this? It is hers—one hundred and ten percent her fault.

If your phone has a higher chance of breaking without a case, why not buy a case? Isn't this common sense? Yes.

While I preach frugality, common sense would dictate that buying a phone case is cheaper than having to pay to constantly have your phone repaired.

This common-sense approach can be applied to so many different things. Checking your car fluids regularly since it lengthens the lifespan of your car. Taking care of your teeth and flossing daily to prevent hundreds of dollars' in dental fees later in life. Staying in on school nights to study so you can pass your test and complete your homework. Drinking your wine at the kitchen table rather than the couch so if you spill something you don't have to worry about paying to get the stain removed. Working multiple jobs throughout college so you don't have years of college debt to pay off after.

Common sense is used in every decision we make. Do I wake up early so I can work out and burn some of this extra fat off, or do I go back to sleep? Should I fill my gas tank up at this gas station even though it's more expensive than the one two blocks away? When it's lunchtime, should I eat the chicken breast I packed or buy a pizza from the cafeteria? After I leave my day job, should I pick up a night shift to help cover rent or go to happy hour with my coworkers?

Everything we do is pushing us toward our goals or pulling us further away. Use common sense and you will begin to see drastic changes in your life. Changes that are well worth it.

WHAT MORE CAN YOU DO?

If it's not broke, don't fix it.

Right around the time the iPhone 10 was coming out, I was still managing to get by with an iPhone 5c. During this same time, I was wearing broken sunglasses, torn up shoes, and Walmart watches.

Yet, they all did the job.

If something continues to serve its purpose, why spend money on a new one? This is common sense isn't it?

When I got my first car in high school, there was nothing I wanted more than subwoofers. Two 12's in the back with a nice amplifier and a new stereo system. Even though this would have been great, it would have been a purchase based on wants, rather than needs.

The car I was using at the time was close to twenty years old, had nearly 200,000 miles on it and wasn't worth more than $1,000. The cost of the new stereo system, subs, amplifier, and installation would have cost more than the car itself was worth.

I had to use a little common sense. By doing so, I separated my wants from my needs. The choice was much clearer, and I shot that idea down just as quickly as it had come up. Wants are endless but needs are necessary. Only buy what you need and moderate your cravings. Use common sense.

HOW TO LAST LONGER: WITH POSSESSIONS, NOT IN BED

Don't procrastinate. If your check engine light comes on, take care of it right away. If your necklace begins to rust, clean it right away. If you have home-work due in a week, do it the night it is assigned. If you have the list of text-books you need to buy, buy them right after class. Don't let your list pile up. Be proactive and stay on top of it. This I would say, is common sense.

Anytime your shoes get muddy and dirty, wash them by hand. Most people have created the habit of cleaning them in the washer and dryer, but this can be harmful to your shoes. It can rip the material, fade the coloration, shrink the fabric, and may even melt the rubber. Instead of carelessly throwing your shoes in the laundry, grab a scrub brush, a dark colored washcloth (so that you don't ruin lighter washcloths with mud, slime, and grime) and a bucket of water. Scrub feverishly!

When buying shoes, keep in mind that darker shoes will appear less worn out over time than a lighter pair. Be smart. Don't buy a shoe because it looks good. Instead, buy a shoe because of its quality. Some shoes don't hold their value. This I would say, is common sense.

Watch what you spend. Go to wholesale stores. Don't eat out. Make your own lunch. Home cook your meals. Don't try and be Mr. Glamorous. Live below your means. Don't exhaust yourself by trying to impress others. Shop at Goodwill and other thrift stores. This I would say, is common sense.

Before making a purchase, ask yourself these things: Do I already have some-thing that can do the job? Can I borrow it from someone I know? Can I trade something for it? Can I make it myself? Can I put this purchase off to a later date? Have I looked for a lower-cost alternative? Have I looked at a thrift store or a consignment shop? Have I looked online for discounts? This I would say, is common sense.

If you can't break away from bad spending habits, then try asking for dis-counts. You can do this anywhere. Fast food joints, movie theaters, thrift stores. Anywhere. You will be pleased to find that there are student discounts at most places you shop. If not, there may be an employee discount that the store representative won't mind giving you. Nobody likes turning others down. It's human nature to want to say yes to others—it's a natural response. Because of this, you'll find that store employees will go ahead and give you a discount to avoid feeling bad for saying no. This I would say, is common sense.

"Common sense is not a gift, it's a punishment, because you have to deal with all the people who don't have it." – Unknown

CHAPTER 17

MONEY DOESN'T GROW ON TREES

During college, I worked ten jobs over a period of four years. I always found ways to make more money. Part of this was the fact that I started working at fourteen and learned the value of a dollar at a young age. Another reason may have been that I wanted to help take some stress off my parents. The rest was probably my need to be different, my hunger to get ahead and my craving for more. But this chapter is not only about me—it's about how I found a way, and how you can too.

This journey to graduating debt-free and getting ahead is not easy. Sacrifices need to be made every day to put yourself in a better position. If you fall seven times, get up eight. If you have two jobs already, find time for a third. Four years of hard work now is nothing compared to sixty years of hard work after college. Follow good habits and you will see good results. Learn to work hard and your life will become easier.

There are so many ways to make money. While in college I worked as a janitor at a movie theater, I hauled Christmas trees during the winter, mowed lawns for neighbors, cleaned trashcans at the park, and even wrote essays for class-mates. I started my own moving company, worked as a valet, and attempted to create an online e-commerce publishing company. I bartended, life-guarded, and chauffeured. Any free time I had was spent trying to find extra ways to make money so that I could pay for college outright.

There are always ways to make money. Excuses like "There are no jobs in this town", "I don't have the time to make money", "Nobody will hire me", or "I can't find any work" are unacceptable.

If the company you apply to work for doesn't get back to you within a week, send a follow up email, dial up the phone and ask to speak with the manager, or walk into the business in person and plead your case. There is no excuse for not getting hired. If you can't find work, rub your eyes, and look again. There are opportunities to make money everywhere.

If there legitimately aren't any jobs in the town you live in, use your brain power and create some. Walk door to door and offer to wash peoples' cars, or offer to clean storefront windows. Offer to pick up dog poop or clean bird poop off railings. Tell jokes door to door for twenty-five cents a laugh. Play Rock-Paper-Scissors with strangers, if they lose, they have to pay you a dollar;

if you lose, you have to call your ex. Get creative—there is rarely a good excuse for not being able to make money.

GET CREATIVE

We are all passionate about something. If not passionate, we are all interested in something.

We enjoy fishing, running, video games, shopping, and make-up. We enjoy movies, working out, singing, or reading. Whatever it is you enjoy; you can make money doing it.

What about sleeping and sitting on the couch all day? You can probably make money doing this too. If you enjoy sleeping, why don't you talk about? Sounds odd, but I guarantee there are other people out there who like to sleep as much as you do. People with similar interests like to listen to similar stories, so start a podcast, YouTube channel, or a blog.

There is something about being relatable that rubs people the right way. You can make money by doing one of these things and telling the world why sleeping is so great and why you enjoy it so much. Once you gain a little following and get some fans, you can start calling yourself the 'Sleeping Stallion' and brand yourself. Next thing you know, your fans will want to buy your 'Sleeping Stallion' merchandise and you're off to the races. Making money off something you love…sleeping!

When I was a freshman in college, I wrote an E-book and published it on the Kindle app through Amazon. My close friend, Greg, and I did this to try and create a form of passive income. We made a whopping $2 off this E-book! Impressive, I know.

But it wasn't how much we made that mattered. Instead, it was more about the fact that we tried.

Later that year, I tried to create an app called Simple-Smile. This app would have allowed people to post nice messages to other users daily with the purpose of spreading positivity. It would also send positive or motivational quotes every morning to start the user's day with positive affirmations. Lastly, it would send out reminders to keep the users accountable towards their goals. In a nutshell, the idea of the app was to be a virtual, affordable life coach.

I continuously tried to start my own businesses. Clothing brands, YouTube channels, dog walking services, landscaping, and moving companies. I offered to install Christmas lights, drive wealthy personnel to dinner parties, power wash driveways, and tried to contract out younger guys to do manual labor.

Most of these endeavors never went anywhere, but what I realized is that there are always opportunities available to make money. Sometimes you just have to create the opportunities yourself. If you have an idea that you think could be something special, don't just chase the dream—catch it! Anyone can start a company, including you. Take a chance!

DIRTY WORK, DIRTY REPUTATION

You can't fear what other people might think of you during the grind. You can't worry about what troubles the grind brings along the way. You can't worry about the time lost when you're making money.

If you're serious about graduating debt-free, you will make time for the grind. The grind will take priority, and the dirty work and the dirty looks won't bother you. You won't mind the sacrifices.

When you chose to make money over going out to party, you will lose friends. This is a fact. The choice is hard at first, but you will see the upside when the numbers in your bank account start to increase. Your relationships will get weaker, but your pockets will get deeper. Your circle of friends will get smaller, but the stack of money will get taller. I promise it will be worth it.

Dirty work, dirty reputation has a double meaning. On one end, it means the decrease in time spent with friends and family, resulting in a less appealing reputation. On the other end, it relates to the pride you should take in your profession, no matter what it is you do to make money.

While I was in high school and college, I wasn't always trying to start publishing companies and iPhone apps. The work I did wasn't always that pretty. Rather, I worked in concession stands, cleaned movie theaters, scrubbed toilets, mopped floors, emptied trashcans, and so much more.

Being seen scrubbing poop off toilets, hauling trash to dumpsters, and removing gum from movie theater seats was tough. It was a blow to my ego unlike anything you could possibly imagine. But I had a bigger vision for my life, and I was willing to do whatever it took to get there—even if that meant scrubbing toilets.

If you don't have the passion to graduate college debt-free, then you will never do it. If you're not willing to have a "by any means necessary attitude", then you will fail. If you don't have the burning desire in your heart to do whatever it takes to graduate college debt-free, then I would highly recommend returning this book right now and reading no further.

You need to create within your head a level of mental toughness that no look, no comment and no criticism can break. When someone says something that is degrading or that belittles you and the hard work you put in every single day, you need to have enough of a wall built up around your heart to not let it bother you.

When it happens, and it will happen, you need to know that what you're doing is all part of a bigger purpose, a bigger plan. Always keep the end goal in sight and remember that you are a beast, you are a warrior, and you will not be broken.

Swallow your pride and make your money. Bartend at Hooters, work as a stripper, clean toilets for commercial sites, mow lawns for the people you know, pick up trash at city parks, mop floors at a grocery store, work as a cashier at McDonalds, donate plasma, pick up dog poop, deliver pizzas, work the graveyard shift for a security company, apply for a construction job, become a plumbers apprentice. Literally do anything.

Then, let this anything become a something. Let it become your something. Take pride in it and be the best damn stripper you can possibly be. Clean toilets like they've never been cleaned before. Pick up trash like a world class garbage man.

Take pride in who you are and remember the bigger picture. The dirty jobs are worth it in the end. The money is worth it in the end. The financial freedom is worth it in the end. Graduating college debt-free is worth it in the end.

Don't let the naysayers get in your head. Do what you have to do so you can graduate college debt-free. And to anyone who has something negative to say about the way you make your money, use these two very effective words to keep them from bothering you again: Fuck off.

"To understand the heart and mind of a person, look not at what he has already achieved, but at what he aspires to." – Kahlil Gibran

OBSESS OVER IT

The first step to making money is creating the desire to get it. Obsession follows the pursuit of passion. Similarly, the desire to graduate college debt-free, and to put yourself ahead of your peers, needs to become a passionate hunger first.

Once you become so focused and engulfed in making money, the universe will work in your favor. Your external reality is created from your internal aptitudes. Therefore, once you begin to discover different ways of making money, you will find that a chamber in your brain unlocks.

This chamber will allow you to begin seeing the world differently. You'll find yourself coming up with mini business ideas in your head, finding ways to make money with the things you see everywhere you go, and you'll realize how easy it is to make money when you allow creativity to flow freely through you. Once you get to this point mentally, you can begin to believe you have already made it, and the universe will force others to begin believing it too.

"The universe will correspond to the nature of your song." – Reverend Michel Beckwith

CHAPTER 18

THE LITTLE THINGS, LITERALLY

PICK UP THE ABRAHAMS.

This pointless little one cent piece of iron is worth a million dollars. Not in monetary value, obviously. But rather, in what the penny represents to most people: insignificance.

Why is that? Is it because it holds the least amount of monetary value of all the coins? Probably so. But if we continue to neglect the little things, we will miss the opportunity of the compound affect.

I'm sure you are all familiar with the magic penny question:

If I offered you $1 million right now or gave you a magical penny that doubled every day for thirty-one days (one month), which would you choose?

Watch what happens to this penny over thirty days!

Day 1	$.01	Day 16	$327.68
Day 2	$.02	Day 17	$655.36
Day 3	$.04	Day 18	$1,310.72
Day 4	$.08	Day 19	$2,621.44
Day 5	$.16	Day 20	$5,242.88
Day 6	$.32	Day 21	$10,485.76
Day 7	$.64	Day 22	$20,971.52
Day 8	$1.28	Day 23	$41, 943.04
Day 9	$2.56	Day 24	$83,886.08
Day 10	$5.12	Day 25	$167,772.16
Day 11	$10.24	Day 26	$335,544.32
Day 12	$20.48	Day 27	$671,088.64
Day 13	$40.96	Day 28	$1,342,177.28
Day 14	$81.92	Day 29	$2,684,354.56
Day 15	$163.84	Day 30	$5,368,709.12
		Day 31	$10,737,418.24

Do you see this? When you take a penny and double it every day for a month that is what you end with—$10.7 million. This is the power of compounding interest. Staying disciplined during college can have the same effect on your life.

Now this is a wild example. The magic penny does not exist in the real world. However, let's say it could be applied to the actions you take in your own life. For example, what if small, daily disciplines could amass to a billion-dollar company or a professional sports career? If others can achieve levels of success as such, I'd argue that you can certainly graduate college debt-free with the same framework in mind.

The same goes for the big job, the perfect attendance award, the 4.0 grade average, the varsity accolades. These are all a result of focusing on the little things.

No great feat is accomplished without attention to detail.

This concept of discipline is also applicable in other ways. During the course of a year, I picked up every penny, nickel, quarter, and dime I saw on the ground. I kept all my spare change and put it into a jar. At the end of the year, I put all my coins in a pile and was amazed with how much I had collected.

Over the one year that I collected spare change, I had a total of $226.18. Enough to pay for more than half of the ten-day road trip I took with my friends to the White Sands, Grand Canyon and Zion National Park.

The trip wasn't luxurious by any means. We bought groceries at Dollar General, ate hotdogs for breakfast, showered in rivers, wore the same clothes multiple days in a row, and spent the night at off-road campsites. But even then, we got to see some of the most beautiful parts of the country on less than $450.

With just a year's worth of picking up spare change, you can have your groceries covered for an entire month, or finally get a new pair of tires. You can buy a present for your mom or treat your dad to a meal. You can invest it in the stock market or pay your utilities for the month. The extra money goes a long way.

LOUISIANA LIVING LEGEND

I once read a story about a Louisiana man who collected pennies for over forty-five years. He filled up over a dozen five-gallon water containers. It took the bank nearly six hours to count all the spare change. In total, he had over a half million pennies. It totaled $5,136.14 which was enough to pay off a recent dental bill.

Imagine, if instead of just pennies, he had collected nickels, dimes, and quarters as well. Maybe even a crumpled-up dollar bill here and there. That number could have easily been closer to $20,000.

Saving extra money is important. No matter how many expenses you have, you should always make it a goal to put away at least ten percent of your paycheck every month. In order to do this, you must budget extremely hard.

Keep track of all your expenses, and toward the end of the year, go back and see how much you spent on unnecessary things like eating out, going to the movies, and spending the weekend at the bar. Then make it a goal to cut back ten percent on those expenses and save everything that is left over.

You'll find that you spent money of clothes you really didn't need, movies you shouldn't have made time for, fast food you shouldn't have ate, and other pointless things that ended up costing thousands of extra dollars.

Learn to become more like this Louisiana Man and remember that it's the little things that make a big difference. Discipline adds up, just like pocket change. By keeping track of what you spend, and saving every chance you get, you'll slowly start inching ahead.

It is the small habits that most people overlook that end up giving us an edge in life. If you learn to capitalize on the little things, you can begin winning the big things. Take control and watch as your life begins to change.

PERCENTAGES

According to CNBC, seventy percent of Americans save less than ten percent of their income every month. Of the thirty percent who do save more than ten percent of their income, the majority of this group is fifty-five and older.

The top ten percent of wealthiest Americans possess more than seventy percent of all the nation's financial assets. Did you notice that these exact numbers are switched? Coincidence? I think not. Here are some stats:

- Top 10% of wealthiest population = 70% of nation's financial assets

- 70% of population = Saves only 10% of income

What's the difference between the top 10% and the rest of the population? The way the wealthy handle their money—proper planning, continuous saving, and smart investing.

- The median millionaire spends $90k a year while earning $250k in income, an impressive 64% savings rate.

The wealthiest ten percent of Americans are avid savers. They invest their saved money in Roth IRA's, growth stock mutual funds, 529's, the stock market, real estate, and low-cost index funds. By continuing to save and investing their money—with the intent of being long term investors—the wealthy exercise their discipline and become millionaires.

Those of you who are willing to do the little things, can follow in these footsteps as well. By continuing to stay disciplined, you will slowly get ahead. This consistency will help you graduate debt-free, become highly successful and maybe even become a millionaire too.

Just because you don't have to work, doesn't mean you shouldn't. Always do those extra little things to help put you ahead.

"It is all the little choices we make every day that make the difference in the world." – Darren Hardy

CHAPTER 19

WORK HARDER & DON'T COMPLAIN

Listed below is a list of ten habits that the world's most successful people do every morning. I want you to take the time to read through these habits and compare your current morning routine with the ones of the CEO's, millionaires, and large business owners of our generation. Place a checkmark next to the habits you currently engage in and mark an 'X' next to the ones you don't.

- Do you wake up between 4am and 7am on a regular basis?

- Do you work out before you start your day?

- Do you take cold showers?

- Do you make your bed?

- Do you meditate?

- Do you read part of a self-help book before the day begins?

- Do you challenge yourself to do one thing that you don't want to do simply for the purpose of personal growth?

- Do you engage in positive affirmations?

- Do you look at your list of goals and visualize yourself accomplishing them?

- Do you write daily lists of what you're grateful for?

If I told you that each of these habits would make you five percent more successful, would you start doing them? Most likely you would because success is exciting. However, without knowing why these routines will make you successful, most of you will get discouraged and stop doing them. So, let's discuss it.

1. Remove The Snooze – Successful people understand time is precious. When their alarm goes off in the morning, they roll right out of bed

and get straight to it. No snooze, no extra sleep. The earlier you wake, the more time you'll have to get one step closer to your goals.

2. Exercise – By exercising for just twenty-three minutes, endorphins in your brain are naturally released which will result in a mood and energy boost for twelve hours. Start your day with exercise to reduce stress, improve your attitude, and increase productivity for the rest of the day.

3. Cold Showers – Cold showers reduce stress levels. Ironically, cold showers impose a small amount of stress on your body. However, this stress leads to a process called hardening which will help your nervous system gradually get used to handling moderate levels of stress. Cold showers will also help wake your body up, as it causes you to take deeper breaths. This decreases carbon dioxide levels throughout the body, helping you concentrate. Cold showers keep you focused and alert throughout the day. They also increase willpower. It takes mental toughness to undergo the cold for extended periods of time. By implementing cold showers into your morning routine, you are building up your mental willpower, which will improve not just the rest of your day, but your entire life.

4. Make The Bed – This may appear to be a small task, but making the bed helps you start the day off right. This simple decision at the start of the day begins a chain of other good decisions throughout the rest of the day.

5. Meditation – Spiritual practices such as meditation or prayer will help you center yourself during the rush of the day. Doing this will give you energy and set positive intentions.

6. Reading – Self-Growth books will help you start to believe you can be more, do more and live a fuller life. Reading a chapter or two before the day starts can give you the inspiration you need to dare yourself to go where you haven't gone before, so you can experience what you haven't had before.

7. Comfort Zone – You have no idea what you're made of until you venture outside of your own familiar world. By doing something challenging at the start of the day, you are pushing yourself to grow.

8. Affirmations – Positive affirmations are very powerful because they release you from negativity, fear, worry, and anxiety. By repeating positive affirmations every morning, you will begin to take charge of your

117

thoughts, slowly changing your pattern of thinking and ultimately changing your life.

9. Visualization – This habit might be the most important of the ten. The law of attraction, states that energy goes where attention flows.

10. Gratitudes – Writing a list of gratitudes every morning is a great way to get yourself in the right frame of mind for the rest of the day. By making a point of writing down who and what you're grateful for in your life, you will begin the day with optimism, which is just another step on the way to success.[6]

Every day you have the responsibility to grow. You have the responsibility to be a better version of yourself today then you were yesterday, and tomorrow than you were today. You can choose whatever it is you want to do and wherever you want to go within your own mind. You create the life that you envision.

The universe will correspond to the nature of your sound. The energy you put out into the world is magnetized and comes right back at you. Therefore, if you chose to be lazy, then your life will be full of lazy people, lazy thoughts, and lazy goals. However, if you chose to be great and commit yourself to success, then your life will be just that.

You can always work harder. You can always become a better version of yourself. There is always room for improvement and growth. Graduating college debt-free is not easy. It takes a lot of willpower. It is stressful working multiple jobs while taking a full course load at school. It is hard saving money when you see a pair of shoes you want or a restaurant you've been craving. It is difficult turning down your friends, or a date, because you have work in the morning. But these tough tasks are necessary, and if you don't learn to sacrifice now, you'll just be another old dog who can't learn a new trick.

"When we believe we can be more, we're pulled to do and feel more." Mark Zuckerberg

WHAT DOES IT TAKE?

Assuming you don't own a renowned digital marketing agency or an e-commerce business that produces a million dollars annually, one of the hardest parts about graduating college debt-free is changing your perception on what

---

[6] https://www.success.com/why-you-should-make-visualization-a-daily-practice/

it takes to get there. For all of you paying your way through college, one job won't be enough. One source of income won't get you there.

When I was in college, my summers were jammed packed with work. I would lifeguard from 5am to 12pm, chauffeur from 1pm to 6pm and then work as a valet attendant from 7pm to 12pm. After all this, I still had homework for my summer classes to take care of, janitorial services to tend to, and a sick father at home.

But for me, this was nothing new. All I had ever known was hard work. This has been my life since eighth grade. I worked on Labor Day, Memorial Day, Thanksgiving. I worked on my birthday, my mom's birthday, my dad's birthday. I worked on Halloween, Easter, and Veterans Day. I worked on Christmas, New Year's Eve and New Year's Day. I worked in the January cold, the August heat, and the May thunderstorms. The grind didn't stop and I credit this consistency to changing my thought patterns.

By changing my thought patterns, and consistently reminding myself that I could always do more and work harder, I continued to take the necessary step needed to graduate college debt-free. I became obsessed with improvement and obsessed with making more money. I had no time to worry about what other people were doing or think about how tired I was after those long workdays. My burning desire to graduate college debt-free kept me pushing forward and I didn't let anyone, or anything, slow me down.

I knew that if I worked hard while I was in college, the rest of my life would be easier. I was wise enough to realize that the 'college chapter' was temporary. The parties, the girls, and the daring fun would fade away just as quickly as it started. I knew that those who used their time to make money, conquer their thoughts, and engage in daily improvement, would graduate not a scholar, but rich in the mind. I knew I could accomplish in just four short years what it would take most people to accomplish in twenty. So, I set out to achieve financial freedom, mental clarity, and an unparalleled work ethic.

I kissed up to managers and worked hours that would drive most people crazy. I laughed at jokes that weren't funny, gave compliments I didn't mean, and forced myself to be around people I didn't care for. The more I sacrificed, the closer I got.

I went from scrubbing toilets as a janitor, to flying across the world as a travel assistant. I went from cleaning hot fryer grease at the movie theater, to sitting beachside in Cabo San Lucas as a medical aide. I went from mowing yards in the Texas summer heat, to living out my dream. I didn't lose sight of the end goal and it worked.

If you truly want something bad enough, you need to work harder today than you did yesterday. There is no such thing as a day off on the path to success. One day off can result in a full week of trying to catch up.

It is important to remember that you can always do more. If seeds are your goals, your thoughts are the water needed to make them grow. What you tell yourself, directly determines the direction and magnitude of your success. The tools you need to graduate college debt-free are already within your mind.

"The more you visualize yourself living the life you want, the sooner universal energies will align with you to give you what you want." – Jacklyn Janeksela

WORK HARDER THAN YOU HAVE TO

In college, I was always looking to make extra money. The movie theater I worked at hosted movie premiers on Tuesday and Wednesday nights. Because they were always understaffed, I was able to pick up extra hours and make more money.

The show times for these new movie releases were always at midnight. After twenty minutes of previews, the movie would begin. They usually lasted anywhere between ninety and 180 minutes. If you do the math, this means I wouldn't leave the movie theater until 3:30am, sometimes four in the morning. If this is what you estimated, you're right; 4am in the middle of the week wasn't uncommon for me.

School would come around the next morning and I'd be falling asleep in class. With hundreds of people coming to the theater to watch these premiers, overseeing the entire concession stand operation was exhausting.

But I never complained.

There is no time to sit around and be lazy. You can't forfeit your time to idle temptations. Time spent sitting around is time wasted. Every chance you get to progress, take it. Push through and push forward. Stop for nobody, stop for nothing. You are capable of so much more than you think.

A few of the paychecks I collected while working at the movie theater between 2013 and 2017.

ONE JOB IS NOT ENOUGH

There are plenty of ways to find an extra job. You can ask the kid who sits next to you in class or the scary guy that sits next to you on the bus. You can ask your professor or your coach, a family member, or a friend. Go to the back of the newspaper and look at the job listings or use the Google search bar on your phone. Use a school computer or go to the public library and look up Craigslist ads. If all fails, hitch a ride to the mall and go from store to store asking for an interview. There are plenty of ways to find a job and no excuse for not being able to get one.

When I was in college, I would make flyers using the school computers. I'd post them around campus or around neighborhoods close to mine offering pet sitting, dog walking, landscaping, car detailing, and power washing services. I always ended up getting dozens of calls. This allowed me to make quick money and proves that you can do the same.

121

All the businesses I started during college in the above picture.

You can do practically anything you want to make money. Offer to pick up dog poop, babysit, or house-sit. You can clean gutters or rake leaves. You can wash windows or help organize garages. You can even set up a lemonade stand with a sign that reads: *Broke college student, please help me out.* I promise you, there are good people out there that will.

There is no excuse for not being able to get a job. There always has been and always will be opportunities to make money. If you don't have kids, don't have a spouse, and don't have criminal charges pending, then being "broke" is just a matter of you not trying hard enough.

It is hard, but no matter the situation you're in, you're never completely stuck. There is a way out. There is a light.

You can't lose hope.

There are good people out there who have been in your shoes. They have struggled with the same things you are dealing with right now and they will help you. You just need to start by making the effort to put yourself out there, work harder, and have faith in your plan. Hard work doesn't go unnoticed. The universal language in this world is toughness and hard work. If you promise to do these two things in life, you will be rewarded. This world can be tough, but it truly is all about what you make of it. Nobody ever regretted working hard.

HARD WORK PAYS OFF

My junior summer of college, I received an amazing opportunity to intern with Henry Schein, the largest distributor of dental supplies in the world. Schein has a presence in thirty-two countries, is a Fortune World's Most Admired Company, ranked number one in its industry for social responsibility by Fortune magazine and sees annual revenues of 13 billion yearly.

Despite working three other jobs and taking summer classes, I still managed to finish as the number one intern in the country. Of the twenty-three interns that were selected nationwide, 3,360 office surveys were submitted, 390 of those surveys were from me.

I had set up more meetings than any other rep in the country and visited more offices. I competed against interns from all over the country—huge cities like Houston, Boston, Chicago, San Diego, and Fort Lauderdale were covered by the other interns in the program. Despite there being more dental offices per capita in some of those areas, those interns still didn't manage to accomplish what I did. I still won.

There is a reason I'm telling you this story. I knew for a fact that I would win for two reasons:

1) My unparalleled work ethic.

2) My unwavering belief.

I would force myself to get up at seven in the morning and submit surveys until seven at night. I worked through the weekends preparing myself for the week ahead. I made extra calls even though I didn't have to, talked to extra offices even though I didn't need to and made extra visits even when I didn't want to.

I wrote personalized thank you cards and dropped off chocolates to all my offices. I put thousands of miles on my car and did what the other interns didn't have the energy for. I knew I would come out on top. I knew that I would win. I believed in myself until my belief became my reality.

When you want something bad enough, don't let anything stop you from getting it. You have the power to make a name for yourself, the power to break generational curses, and the power to be the best in your industry. But if you don't work hard, none of this is possible. I encourage you all to take the lessons from this chapter and apply them to your own life. No excuses, only hard work and discipline. You can do it—take that first step!

"By failing to prepare, you are preparing to fail." – Benjamin Franklin

CHAPTER 20

IMAGINE WORKING HARDER

Imagine waking up one hour earlier every single day. That's 365 extra hours of time that could be spent working towards your goals, rather than dreaming about them. That is 365 extra hours to grow and develop your skills. That is 365 extra hours to make money and that is 365 extra hours to plan how you're going to graduate college debt-free.

You will never accomplish your goals by sleeping in. If you're not a morning person, become one. Idle time is your worst enemy and laziness is the biggest roadblock on the path to success.

There are no cheat codes to getting ahead. It all comes down to how hard you work and how badly you want it. You must have a burning desire to win, a burning desire to achieve and a burning desire to graduate college debt-free. Once you have this burning desire, graduating college debt-free will simply become a byproduct to your larger success.

You should always be the hardest working person in the room. If you sense that someone is working harder than you, then you need to reassess and fix your work ethic immediately. If someone were to ask you the question, "Who is the hardest working person you know?" The answer should always be yourself, nobody else.

When you work hard, money becomes an endless spring of water. It flows into your life with ease and abundance—money will practically fall into your lap. You will attract money. You will be a money-magnet. No matter what you do, money will keep pouring into your life.

DON'T FALL INTO THE STEREOTYPE

I'm going to sound like a baby boomer here, but it is the truth: Kids these days don't want to work hard. You hear all too often old timers saying it, but they are speaking facts. We don't see go-getters anymore and that is part of the reason the college debt epidemic is a thing. Yes, prices of tuition have skyrocketed, but when has a little adversity paralyzed young Americans?

We've gone through two World Wars, the Great Depression, Civil Rights movements, the ME movement of the 70s and the age of anxiety in the 90s.

Yet, for the first time, young Americans feel stuck, in a rut, helpless. Young Americans go to college to be successful, which statistically does provide an advantage. But once they go, they run into problems paying for it afterwards. For some, it takes over twenty years to get out of this money madness.

It is important to keep your mental game in check. Whining and complaining does nothing for you. Feeling bad for yourself gets you nowhere. Pick your chin up and keep moving forward.

"Out of adversity comes opportunity." – Benjamin Franklin

SEEK DISCOMFORT

If you're not committed to self-development, you're committed to self-destruction. There is no middle ground. It is either moving forwards or moving backwards. When you stop, you're not staying in one spot like you think you are. Instead, you're moving down the ladder of success because others are moving up it, leaving you behind.

Stop following the crowd.

You don't have to go out every Friday and Saturday night. You don't have to buy the newest video game or the latest line of clothing. You don't have to work at the same place as all your friends. You don't have to graduate college with debt like everyone else. It's time you started taking ownership of your life. It's time you started leading the pack and creating a path for others to follow. Be true to yourself and be true to your goals.

The easy road often becomes hard and the hard road often becomes easy.

During college, no matter how tough things got, I continued to push forward. I quickly realized that the hardest things to do, often prove to help us get the furthest ahead. Even as my life started to noticeably change for the better, others around me still couldn't understand my vision. They didn't understand why I was working so hard, why I never went out, and why I had such an urgency to grow up.

They questioned all my hours of hard work as they binge-watched Netflix. They questioned all the nights I stayed at home as they partied until the sun came up. They thought my work ethic was unnecessary and a waste of time.

Now, they ask how? How did you graduate college debt-free? How did you write a book? How did you already make six figures at twenty-one? And all I can say is the answer was right in front of them the whole time.

"At first they will ask why you're doing it, later they'll ask how you did it." – Unknown

DON'T PUT IT OFF

You have to cut others off while you're on the path to success. If your friends are holding you back, it's time to find new ones. If your friends can't see out your vision, find those that can. You need to surround yourself with others that are trying to grow and get better every day. Don't settle for less when you know deep down you are worth so much more.

During winter, summer, and spring break I had friends that would say, "You're on break from school, man. You can take it easy!" They tried to convince me that I could relax and hangout with them since school was over with. But accepting laziness into my life was not an option. These friends were using the break as an excuse to stray away from the grind.

You can't cheat yourself during this grind. You have to put in the time. You have to put in the hours. The only way you'll make it is by truly giving it your all. You have to respect the process because graduating college debt-free doesn't happen overnight.

I think one of the hardest things in the world is doing something that is extremely hard, knowing that you have the choice to stop. The strongest people are the ones that push themselves when they don't have to. They simply do it for the challenge and for the thrill of accomplishment.

This hunger for growth is what separates the men from the boys, the winners from the losers. It is the decision to continue pushing, even though you have the option to stop, that separates the great from the average.

If you're not doing the most productive thing at every possible given moment, then you're not working hard enough.

If you know better, then why don't you decide to do better? Because it's hard? Everything can change depending on what you do today. Everything can change depending on what you do right now. You have to live with every decision you make. Why don't you make it easier on yourself and do what you know is right?

Jocko Willink said it best. "More discipline equals more freedom." You must give up what you want now, to get what you want later. Don't put off until tomorrow what you can do today.

Decide what you want for yourself, then don't let anything get in the way. There's no easy way out. Create more discipline for yourself and raise your standards. Unleash your mighty power and dare to be great.

QUICK MOTIVATION

For the Couch Potatoes who sit around all day waiting for something great to happen. To the Sofa Spuds who complain about not having enough money. To the Slouchers who can't seem to find a job that pays them enough. To the Chair Warmers who claim there's not enough time in the day, and to the Lazy Larry's who whine about being broke, about all the homework they have, and about the weight they've put on, grow up.

There isn't time for any of this. Don't be a complainer. Don't make excuses. Learn to love pain. Learn to love the struggle. Learn to let all the things that are working against you help you grow.

Nobody wants to see that you're going to be more successful than they are. Everyone wants to be the best. But you have to dig deep and find the drive, the strength, and the toughness inside you to get past all of this.

If your friends can't keep up, then find new ones. Don't slow down for anyone. Nobody can stop you. You are a freight train moving forward, crushing anything in your path. You are a strong leader with a great mindset. You have a drive like no other. You are one of a kind.

You are strong-willed. You are hungry. You're a beast. You display grit and resilience daily. When times get hard, you work harder. You don't get discouraged. You take the extra step. You put in the extra effort. You put in the additional hours. You will graduate college debt-free. See it, feel it, know it. You are second to none.

There is a lion mentality inside you ready to be let lose. The world is not prepared for the incredible things you are going to do. Your power and potential are limitless. You will make a name for yourself; it will be remembered.

The world will come to know your story. You just have to continue grinding, working hard, and staying focused. Don't look for excuses. Don't look for an easy way out. Just keep moving forward—one day at a time.

"If you're searching for that one person that will change your life, look in the mirror."—Unkown

LEAVE YOU WITH THIS

When life hits you hard and makes you fall to your knees, it is your response that shapes your future. Don't get stuck in these moments of darkness. Get up and keep moving forward. Teach yourself to love adversity. It's these weeks of constant hecticness, work, and pain, that will make you feel the most alive. It's these moments that will help you grow the most.

Change is inevitable, growth is optional. Take complete ownership over your life. If you aren't happy with where you're at, then get to work. You are the co-creator of your own destiny. You, and only you, are responsible for what comes next.

"You can't have a million-dollar dream with a minimum wage work ethic." – Zig Ziglar

CHAPTER 21

STOP MAKING EXCUSES

Excuses are a coping mechanism to make people feel better about themselves. Excuses help us make peace with failed expectations, help us explain away why we just aren't good enough, and keep us ignoring our lack of effort. But excuses are like eating a piece of cake. You feel good while you do it, but ultimately it drags you down—extra fat, extra sugar, extra carbs.

Excuses keep us stuck in limbo. We can't accomplish our dreams, meet our goals, or live a life of fulfillment when we make excuses. They prevent us from moving forward. Excuses limit our potential and drag us further away from our goals. The more excuses you make, the less you'll accomplish.

"I'm too tired", "There aren't any good jobs in this town", "I don't have the time for it". These are all terrible excuses. If you don't have the time for it, make the time for it. If you're too tired, then drink some coffee. If there aren't any good jobs in your town, then you're not looking hard enough. There are always ways to make money and always ways to save money.

If you're "broke", then it's because you're not working hard enough or not budgeting correctly. If you're unhappy, then it's probably because you keep telling yourself you're unhappy. You are in the position you are in because of the decisions you've made. Nobody is to blame but yourself.

Excuses don't fit on the road to success. Stop yourself before an excuse comes out of your mouth. It's your responsibility to take control. Your future depends on the decisions you make now. The people you befriend, the money you earn, the happiness you experience. Once you believe this and truly get this through your head, the world will be your oyster.

"Tough times don't last, but tough people do." – Robert H. Schuller

YOU AND ONLY YOU

I wish I could sit here and be the one to tell you how to stop making excuses and start going after whatever it is you dream to be in life, but I can't. I can't be the one who motivates you to get out of bed earlier in the morning or helps you party less. I can't be the one who reminds you that you can break generational curses or that you have unlimited potential. All I can do is hope that one day you will realize this yourself, because, it must be you. It has to be you.

Spending more money than you have doesn't cut it. Working less won't cut it. Going out every weekend won't cut it.

It's time to get to business. Time to pick up the pace. Time to work harder than you've ever worked before. Time to trust the process. Time to unleash your inner greatness. Time to rise like a phoenix and never look back. It is time to leave your legacy.

"If you are not getting better you are getting worse"- Joe Paterno

WHAT ARE YOU AFRAID OF?

You shouldn't be afraid of leaving people behind, letting go of old habits, or moving on from toxic environments. If you truly want to get ahead, you can't get attached to the old you. You can't get attached to what's comfortable. You can't cling to the past—it's a trap. The only freedom from what is, is looking forward to what is still to come.

We don't have to stay where we start. We all have a choice to move forward. Don't seek pity from others or play the victim card. We are dealt the hand we are dealt for a reason. It's convenient to blame others for the things that are tough in our lives. However, you must stop this. Instead, take ownership of your life.

If you're upset with who you used to be, or how others used to see you, then that's good. There is no better revenge than success. Use your past mishaps and slip-ups as motivation. In order to stand out, you have to do different and you have to be different.

"There's nothing more powerful than a change in mindset." – Les Brown

THE SECRET TO SUCCESS

There is no secrets to success. It is a result of proper preparation, hard work, and learning from failure. Do you have what it takes?

As others party, work your ass off. As others sit around, grind until the sun comes up. As others have their fun, plan your future. There is no time to waste. You can't get ahead by doing what is comfortable and easy.

You need to know the difference between enjoying your youth and destroying your future. Instead of watching Netflix, read books and expand your business knowledge. Study the minds of the highly successful. Do everything in your power to follow the advice of those that have come before you.

If you don't want to be average, don't do average things. Push your limits and test how far you can go mentally, physically, and spiritually. Take the road less traveled. God has more in store for you.

The best investment you will ever make is in yourself. Be so busy in improving yourself that you have no time to criticize others. Lower your standards for no one, go with what you have, and no matter how rough the pain, you keep standing.

Work while they sleep.

Learn while they party.

Save while they spend.

Live like they dream.

You have nothing to lose, only wins to gain. With desire comes self-motivation, with self-motivation comes hard work; and with hard work comes success. If you don't quit, God won't quit. You too, will get yours soon. Be patient.

"Smooth seas do not make skillful sailors." – African Proverb

BE A STUDENT OF LIFE

Every day you have the chance to grow. Allow the trials and tribulations of life to be your teacher. As a student, take whatever life throws at you gracefully. Even in the most stressful days, life is trying to teach you something. Have a welcoming frame of mind and be open to the lessons of the universe.

This frame of mind will allow you to be a king among men. Changes will quickly take place in your life. You will no longer fit in, but instead, you'll stand out. During your transformation, you will feel like everything is coming together for your highest good. The person you were in the past will be a different person than you are today. Embrace the changes and enjoy the journey that you were always destined to take.

"Precisely on you depends tomorrow."– Pope John Paul ll

LIFE IS HARD

Life is hard. But you have to learn to love the struggle, the process, and the grind. If you can't do that, you will never make it. You will always give up before you reach the finish line.

Become a firm believer that you are the hardest working person in the world and that your hustle can't be matched. Become so utterly focused on your goals, that nothing and no one can get in the way. Push forward regardless of the support from those closest to you. Don't seek approval or outside reassurance. This frame of mind will allow you to stay focused without letting outside opinions discourage your efforts.

Life doesn't happen to you; it happens for you. You can either use the struggle to get stronger and grow or you can continue to complain and be stuck. You can either be a student to life and learn from the hard times or you can act as if you already know it all. There is always room for improvement and always room for growth. Choose wisely.

"What we fear doing most is usually what we most need to do."- Ralph Waldo Emerson

INSPIRATION

One of my favorite Gary Vee episodes is #223 with Eric Thomas. Gary talks about how children from lower income families are at a disadvantage in society, but they are at an advantage when it comes to the hunger for more. Gary went on to explain that a hustler's mentality comes from a dark place deep within.

Without adversity, people don't have the chance to callus. This callusing is vital to our future success in that it is what helps us build resistance to the hard times we inevitably face.

The more adversity we face, the more chips we add to our shoulder. The less adversity we face, the less we have to prove to the world. This struggle breeds great things. Without having experienced genuine adversity before, it's hard to keep fighting when times get tough. It is difficult to achieve great feats in the absence of hardship because the path to paradise is oftentimes through the darkest places.

"Adversity lies at the heart of success." – John C. Maxwell

BY ANY MEANS NECESSARY

I am a huge rap fan. The hard-hitting bass, the rhythms of swagger, and the melodies of pride all put me in a zone unlike any other. I can put rap music in my ears and tune out the rest of the world for hours. It gets me pumped up, motivates me, and helps me stay focused. But I also like rap for a deeper reason.

I cannot compare my life to those who live in the projects, to those who deal with horrific adversity, or to those who face racial prejudice daily. However, the pain in their stories, in their rhymes and in their art, resonates with me.

I've received a lot of my inspiration to push through the hard times in life from rap songs because of their stories of struggle. Their lives of drug dealing, jugging, and living the way of the streets is not matter of choice, but rather of survival.

The cards that they were dealt were so bad that they rarely have any other choice but to join into a life of criminal activity. The pressures of older gang members, the lust for a better life, and the need to put food on their plate, makes it difficult to not get involved. There aren't any promises in the outside world when you're a young minority in the ghetto. So, sometimes it's just easier to join the street life knowing there's a place you'll be supported.

This way of life isn't something you see in the suburbs. People in the projects are fighting for their lives every day. This "by any means necessary" lifestyle has inspired me.

Rappers hustle out of necessity. They hustle to try to get out of the projects and make a name for themselves. They hustle to survive. They hustle because they're desperate for someone to give them a chance. The pain and desperation in their voice is something that I've always felt.

Since an early age, I've always been hungry for more. Hungry to prove myself, to get better and to heighten my family system. I wanted to progress and evolve so I could provide a better life more my kids when the time came.

Rappers inspire me because they also don't want to follow their family history line. They don't want to be a product of their environment. They envisioned something bigger for their life. They changed the way they saw themselves and then the world started to do the same. They defied all odds and prevailed against gang violence, unjust law enforcement, and life in the streets. They made it out. So, can you.

The thought of college debt may feel like shackles around your ankles. You may feel like you're suffocating in debt. But don't forget, you have the power to change this.

If you continue to work hard and make money, continue to look for extra jobs to get by, and continue to do the little things and save, you will make it out. Use the chips on your shoulder as motivation for a better future, welcome a by any means necessary attitude and live like your life depends on it, because it does!

"We must make temporary sacrifices for long term satisfaction." – Shanice Martin

CHAPTER 22

F**K VIDEO GAMES

Imagine this. You're playing a video game, then I walk into the room. I grab your gaming system, unplug it, pick it up, walk it out of the room, through the house, out the front door, into the middle of the street, raise it over my head and slam it onto the ground. Then, I walk into your house, grab a bat, walk back outside, and beat it until there are a million little pieces all over the street. Then as you sit there crying like a baby, I come and comfort you, and tell you that I only did it because I care about you. This ladies and gentlemen is love.

Video games are a waste of time. You may dislike the sound of that, but I'm here to help you graduate college debt-free, not be the carnival ride attendant making sure you have a good time.

Video games are addicting because they're fun. They are a way to take a break from the stresses of the day. An escape from reality. A way to decompress and relax. This stuff is all great, but everything is played in a virtual world. Not the real world.

A world in which the checkpoints reached, the houses built, the money made, and the accomplishments gained, are all for nothing. Nothing but bragging rights to the other low life's that also waste away their days in front of a TV screen.

Put the controller down, turn the gaming system off and step away from the TV. Do something productive rather than locking yourself in your room all day and night. Go outside and take a hike, go workout at a gym nearby, spend some time with your family, go wash your car, read a book, or get another job.

It's bad that video games cost money but it's worse that they cost extra time. Extra time that can be spent contributing to your own life. The achievements earned, and accomplishments made in the world of video games are all superficial. Another point, score, star, or win is not a win in life, but a win in the life of an electronic device that is impeding on your growth.

By playing video games, you are living out someone else's dream, not your own. You are in a realm of dormant stagnancies in which there is no sign of progress, only regress. You and your virtual world character may be the biggest, fastest, and strongest, but in real life you have absolutely no power.

The only way you can change this is by giving up video games. Video games won't help you get ahead. Video games won't help you get any stronger or wealthier, and video games certainly won't help you graduate college debt-free.

I understand there are ways to make money through video games. I get that if you're good enough there are competitions that you can enter. However, to get to this point, you have to be an expert. You must be the best of the best. You must put in your 10,000 hours and practice daily. But if you want to graduate college debt-free, you won't have time for all this. So, at this point, it's just a waste.

Don't pay for games or gaming systems. Save your money and use this extra time to work on yourself, your social skills, and your mindset. This will pay dividends.

"Winners have two basic tricks up their sleeve, and they are very simple. The first one is that winners use their time affectively. The second, winners concentrate on what has to be done and ignore the non-essentials". - Unknown

CELL PHONE ADDICTIONS

Cell phones are addicting. There is no denying that. I'll be the first to admit that I am at fault of being on my phone way more than I should be. I think most of us can agree on this. I also think most of us can come to agree that phones, when used properly, are an amazing tool. However, this is rarely the case.

We don't use our phones just to call Grandma Rosie, just to map ourselves to work and back, or just to calculate the numbers on our math homework. We don't use our phones just to text our boss at work, just to track our heart rate, or just to track stocks and keep up with the news. While these may all be things that we do, there is always a twist.

Instead of calling back your Grandma whom your mom has been angrily getting onto you about for the past three weeks, you call your friend because you're trying to put off homework. Instead of using your phone to map yourself to work and back, you're using your map to look up how far the winner of Bachelor Season 6 lives from you. Instead of using your phone to calculate the numbers on your math homework, you're using your phone to calculate your end of semester GPA to figure out if you'll be able to pass Accounting class. Instead of using your phone to text your boss or professor, you're sending silly memes and GIFs to your group text because Chad cheated on Hannah. Instead of using your phone to track your heart rate, you use it to take Snapchat selfies to show everyone you work out. Instead of using your phone to track stocks and keep up with the news, you overindulge in social media, which leads to another alarming problem.

Social media is an ever-changing entertainment platform filled with funny and interesting content. Internet personalities have created a wave of entertainment unlike anything before. Additionally, users now have an unlimited amount of content to choose from. Search and discovery algorithms make getting tired of watching videos harder than ever before. There is always good content on the homepage and the recommended videos are always bait for more watch time.

We can never get enough, and its ruining lives.

These time-draining internet fisherman take away from our chance to get ahead. Our chance to make extra money and our chance to be ultra-productive. We overindulge in these amenities and slowly spend less time working hard, working out and working towards our goals. In this case, the goal to graduate college debt-free.

In order to graduate college debt-free, you can't lose focus. You can't give in to the temptations of social media. Instead, you must stay far, far away.

When you are on the road to success you must have tunnel vision. You must be so busy improving yourself, that you have no time to judge the things that other people are doing. Your attention must be selective and your vision forward seeking. You don't have any time to waste!

"We feel that we do not have enough time, and yet we waste the precious time we have on video games, text messaging, reading about the lives of talentless celebrities, and spending more money to buy things we don't need." – Karl Pillemer

REMOVE THE DISTRACTIONS

Once I graduated college, I deleted all social media platforms. Looking back, I wish I had done this much earlier. Social media was impeding on my growth, so had to let it all go—Snapchat, Twitter, TikTok, Bumble, Tinder, all of it.

It was ironic seeing the more disconnected I got, the more connected I felt. In other words, the more disconnected I got with the outside world, the more connected I felt within myself. It was a breath of fresh air and I've never been happier.

For anyone trying to free themselves from all the outside noise, I'd highly recommend deleting social media. It is a liberating feeling. If you want clarity in life and a clearer vision, deleting social media can help you do this.

By freeing yourself from the eyes of the world, you can focus on what is important to you and not what is important to your audience.

Don't let the success of others deter you from accomplishing your own goals. Don't let the progress of others discourage you from the progress you've been making in your own life. Let go of social media and reconnect with yourself. Life is too short to waste our time fantasizing about the lives of others.

QUICK MOTIVATION

What has Netflix done for you? Has it made you any money? Has it paid your bills? Has it pushed you to get into the gym? Has it inspired you to be the best possible version of yourself? Has it inspired you to work harder? I think not. I don't think watching TV or watching YouTube all day has done this either. How about video games? Have they helped make you a more productive person? I doubt it.

Maybe it's time you get off your damn computer, off your damn couch and out of your damn bed. Maybe it's time you go out and make something of yourself. Maybe it's time you unlock your true potential and discover what you're capable of.

Get up off your butt and grind. Push yourself to your limit. Do things you don't want to do and don't need to do, simply for the sake of growth. Grow and become obsessed with growth. Crave growth. Itch for growth. Start working towards your future and your kids' future. Begin training your mind to get out of your comfort zone.

Success begins with a commitment to excellence. You need to commit 110 percent of yourself to getting better every day, to breaking old habits and picking up positive ones.

Put down the remote control and pick up a book. Put down the video game controller and pick up a shift at work. Put down the drinks and pick up a gym membership. Put down the fast food and pick up a meditation routine. Put down the old you and pick up the new you.

You can and you will see improvements if you just try.

CHALLENGE: Give up video games for a month and pick up a different hobby that doesn't not involve sitting in front of a screen. This can be biking, hiking, reading, sewing, or working out. Watch as you begin to feel healthier, happier, and more productive. Box up your gaming system and put it in a place where it's out of sight and out of mind. Then take a picture of it and post the picture on social media with the hashtags #gettingahead and #ultraproductive.

CHAPTER 23

NO SLOWING DOWN

I think we can all admit that it is easy to be lazy. It is easy to hit the snooze button. It is easy to stay under the warm, fluffy, cozy covers. It is easy to pick up your phone and browse through social media. It is easy to sit on the couch and watch TV. It is easy to hop on YouTube and watch funny videos.

But it's also easy to be motivated.

It's easy to watch a video or listen to a podcast on Eric Thomas, Tony Robbins, Gary Vee, David Goggins, or Jocko Willink, and be inspired to do something great.

What is hard, is executing. Putting that motivation to action. Taking that first step. Waking up at 5am every morning. Ignoring the phone call to hang out with your friends. Taking that extra job. Doing an extra rep. Saving that extra money.

Everyone wants to be great. Everyone is motivated or can be motivated to be great. But the ones that truly become great, are the ones that execute. The beautiful thing about execution is that we thrive off momentum. The hardest part is starting. The second hardest part is staying consistent. But once you take the first step and once you commit to consistent action, you've started mastering the art of getting ahead.

Consistency turns into habits and habits shape our lives. Habits are the driving force behind our success or failure. This driving force is what allows us to accomplish all the wonderful things we've always imagined doing.

Once you are inspired and motivated, momentum leads the way. You will become so engulfed in your goals that nothing will be able to stop you. You'll become a massive snowball, that gathers more snow and speed, as you roll down the mountain toward your dreams, goals, and aspirations.

Every decision we make matters. Right now, matters. Your choices either push you closer to your goals or pull you further away. Even something as simple as taking a nap after a long day of work rather than cleaning your kitchen is pulling you further from your goals. Become obsessed with the now, obsessed with every little choice you make and keep the momentum rolling forward.

WHO'S STANDARDS ARE YOU LIVING

We're all at fault when it comes to using the phrase, "but everybody does it," to justify an unjust action. Late nights and sleeping in on the weekends are acceptable because everyone does it, right? You're young so its normal to go out and have fun because all the other kids your age do it, right? You've had a long week of work, you deserve to take tomorrow off, right? You got a promotion, it's okay to celebrate all night and skip the workout in the morning, right?

Sure, I do believe in rewarding yourself for accomplishing something important to you. I also believe in balancing work and play as much as you can. But who claims that "everybody does it?" Who makes these rules? Society.

What is society? The majority. And we are trying to be different, right? We're trying to separate ourselves from the masses and master the art of getting ahead so we can graduate college debt-free, aren't we?

To be different, you have to work different. To graduate college debt-free, you can't accept these norms. You can't let the voice of society dictate your choices and make you comfortable. Stop following these rules. Stop following the crowd. Do things your own way and create your own path.

"I watched where everyone was going and went the other way." - Unknown

TODAY, TOMORROW & YESTERDAY

There are three things people rarely regret: waking up early, working out and making money. Sleeping in takes away from the potential to make extra money, getting closer to achieving your fitness goals and the chance to be better today than you were yesterday. If you can get up before the rest of the world is awake, you can get so much done. Every second of everyday matters.

Anyone who has done well for themselves knows that it didn't happen overnight. It was a combination of thousands of small productive decisions. Every choice, every step, every second mattered. They trained themselves to be ultra productive and executed.

What most young adults don't realize, is their concept of hard work, is not hard work. True hard work is tripling what you currently believe hard work to be. You don't know what hard work is. You think you do, but you don't.

Working hard and being productive isn't a couple of hours of going balls to the wall. It is a mindset. A change in the way you look at life, a change in the way you walk, you talk, you act. Hard work is a change in the way you live. Hard work is a change in priorities. Hard work is a change in friends and family, in school and job.

Hard work is giving every single day 110 percent and treating every single day as if it is your last. It is the mindset that the rest of your life depends on today. You won't know what true hard work is until you get to college and have to pay for your rent, utilities, phone bill, car insurance and tuition yourself. You won't know what true hard work is until you work 70 hours a week. You won't know what true hard work is until you sacrifice your college experience to graduate college debt-free. But it's time to learn and prepare for it, because hard work is the main ingredient needed to get ahead.

"The 40% Rule: Navy Seals - When your mind is telling you that you're done, that you're exhausted, that you cannot possibly go any further, you're only actually 40% done." – David Goggins

NEVER GIVE UP

I stand up when I eat breakfast. Why? Because I am always in a rush to get from one place to the next. Always in a rush to hustle and find that next job, that next paycheck, that next source of income.

In college, I always tried to do the most productive thing at every possible moment. During my summers, all the kids that lived at my apartment complex would go to the pool to tan, relax and drink. Every time I went, I brought nothing but a self-help book and water. I sat by myself and read.

As they picked up their drinks, I picked up my book. I did things like this to separate myself from the rest of the kids my age. I worked differently to be different. I wanted to make something of myself. I wanted to be special, so I was willing to do whatever it took to support my continued growth.

I missed out on a lot in college. I didn't get the normal college experience. There came a point where I felt like a lot of my days were on repeat. Every day was the same thing. I was going through the motions. Wake up, go to class, go to work, workout, sleep. Over and over. A puppet to the college debt epidemic.

I felt like I had no control over my situation. Like I had no other choice but to continue doing exactly what I was doing, just to get by. Some of the days felt like they would never end. But they did. Then a semester would end. Then a year would end. Then college ended. And I graduated college debt-free. And I sat in the middle of that auditorium with my cap and gown on, with one emotion: I was proud.

The four-year grind. The early mornings and the long nights. The eleven jobs, the sack lunches, the sobriety, the living at home, the going to community college and the refusal to quit finally paid off. I never gave up. I kept going. I kept standing. I lived through weeks of darkness. I dealt with my demon's head on. I looked at the gates of hell and triumphed.

For everyone out there making sacrifices to get ahead. Keep plowing. You are on the right path. Push and fight through those cloudy days because it doesn't rain forever. You'll be surprised at what the human mind is capable of. You'll be surprised at what you're capable of. Continue to push through and you'll be proud too. I guarantee it.

Where there's a will, there's a way. Don't complain about what you don't have or what you can't do. Don't complain about what you're missing out on or the people that are mad you turned them down. They don't understand. They'll never understand. You have to be willing to give up everything to graduate college debt-free. Your best days are ahead.

"The two most important things in life are to one) work hard and two) not complain about working hard." – Unknown

WHEN YOU'RE FEELING UNMOTIVATED

Every day is a struggle. Right now, is a struggle. But it doesn't always have to be this way. Don't make your future harder on yourself by being lazy now. Don't make it harder on yourself by neglecting the things you know you should do now.

Idle time really is our worst enemy. Nobody succeeds in life by being stagnant. Nobody succeeds in life by sitting around. Nobody succeeds in life by making excuses, whining, or complaining.

During college, you need to push yourself to be productive 24/7. Between drives from home and school or school and work, listen to podcasts on how to save money, how to make money, how to build mental resistance, how to be the best version of yourself, how to be a leader, and how to work harder.

By feeding your mind with this content you will stay hungry and focused. It will keep you dialed into the right frame of mind. It will remind you that others have it worse and you have no excuse to whine and complain. Instead, only a million reasons to work even harder.

Put your head down and drive forward. Lower your shoulder and deliver the hit. Keep moving your feet no matter how heavy life gets. Remove the off switch and push through the rainy days, the struggle, and the hard times. The word surrender is not in your language.

LET THE UNIVERSE TALK

The next time you're in your car alone. Go to YouTube and type in motivational orchestra. As the music begins to play, focus on your breathing, and relax fully. While still staying focused on the road, let go of all the thoughts in your mind and let the music take over. Continue to breathe deeply and watch as your body floods with emotions. You'll finish the car ride inspired and refreshed.

Do this anytime you feel lost, hopeless, or confused. Do this anytime you feel unmotivated. Do this anytime you've lost your drive. Do this anytime you're questioning the purpose of all your hard work. Do this anytime you're close to giving up. Do this anytime you're exhausted and not sure you can keep going. Do this anytime your beliefs are wavering. Do this as often as you can.

This meditation will remind you why you started. A quick refresher of the mind, so you can jump right back into the grind. Right back into the endless days, weeks, and months of productivity. And right back into working towards graduating college debt-free. Take a breath and listen to the universe cheering you on.

DISTRACTIONS

You can't cheat your way to prosperity. There is no short cut. It's all a matter of self-discipline and hard work. You must focus on being productive instead of being busy, be intentional with your time, and only put your energy toward the stuff that will help you win.

Distractions Determine Direction

OR

Discipline Determines Direction

You choose.

Don't be ordinary. Be extraordinary. If the rest of the population zigs, then you zag. Be different, be uncommon. Be the guy that says no. Don't be the guy that goes along with the crowd just to be like everyone else. Dominate life.

What matters in life is not that we didn't win, get the job, or get an A on the test, but rather the fact that we showed up. Sometimes in life the hardest thing to do is show up. We were there despite the rain, there despite the bad weather, and there even though it would have been easier to stay at home. That's growth.

NO SLOWING DOWN

The people that achieve greatness don't have a stop or slow down button. They don't pause or take breaks. Eric Thomas, world class motivational speaker, wakes up every morning at 3am. Mark Cuban, billionaire, wakes up at 5am and still works fifteen-hour days. For super-performers, it is always go, go, go.

Time is our most valuable commodity. We can get more money, but we can't get more time. So, work hard and charge ahead every minute you can. You will pay for every minute you waste. You control what you are going to become.

Be hungry for more. Be hungry to improve your future. Never feel bad for investing in yourself. If you want something, get after it right away and don't procrastinate. If you wait, it may never happen. This is your life and you only get one. So, what are you going to do with the time you have left?

CHAPTER 24

CONQUER YOUR THOUGHTS

You are the master of your mind. The things you tell yourself and the subconscious thoughts that bounce around in your head, become your reality. The person you tell yourself you are, is the person you become. By telling yourself things are hard, things will be hard. By telling yourself you are incapable of achieving your goals, you will never achieve them. It is the thoughts you feed your mind that shape your future. Our only limitations are those we create ourselves.

We are the sole conductor of our thoughts. If we let positive thoughts manifest, success will come. What you feed your mind will shape your future. Turn a deaf ear to the old voices and make new choices. Don't wish it were easier, wish you were better. Never say I can't. Rise up and be great.

The path you take in life is a direct reflection of your current state of mind. Don't let the butterfly effect take you down a path of destruction when you have the capacity to be great. You can be anyone you want to be. Believe in yourself.

Engage in positive affirmations daily. Make these affirmations thorough and specific. If you want to gradate college debt-free, then tell yourself you will graduate college debt-free. If you want a job that pays more money, then tell yourself you will find one that pays more money. The energy you put out into the world comes right back to you.

This is why it is important to learn how to master your thoughts. By training your mind to get comfortable in the uncomfortable, you will always be on a more positive thought frequency. The situations that you never thought you had control of, are the same ones that if conquered, will give you more power over the mind.

One way I was able to do this, was by training my mind daily. I believed that if I consistently practiced doing what was uncomfortable, I'd master my thought patterns. Sure enough, I began to have better control over my thoughts when things got difficult.

Every day for months, I'd keep the AC in my car off even though it was over 100 degrees outside. This may sound ridiculous and a bit reckless, but I did it for the same reason I took ice cold showers all throughout the winter. I did it for the same reason that I'd continue running sprints until my legs gave out. The same reason I'd stay awake longer than I had to and put mental strain on my mind when I didn't need to.

I continued to push my mind and body to its limit. I knew that in order to get where I wanted to be, I needed to train myself to get comfortable in the uncomfortable. I needed to train my mind and I needed to do things that I didn't want to do simply for the purpose of growth.

By training my mind, everything that once seemed hard, became easy. It was all the little things I did daily and consistently, when nobody else was watching, that helped make me stronger. These little challenges changed the entire way I live my life.

It was these moments of adversity that helped me build character, better manage stress, and have more power over my thoughts. This callousing of my mind changed my attitude when times got hard. Instead of giving up easily, I built up a warrior's mentality.

When life delivers a punch and I feel like I can't go any further I smile, because I know deep down, I'd rather die than give up the fight. And through this experience I learned that at my darkest hour, when I stand face to face with who I really am, I know I have what it takes to conquer my thoughts. Do you?

"It is only in our darkest hours that we may discover the true strength of the brilliant light within ourselves that can never, ever, be dimmed." – Doe Zantamata

VELOCITY

Remember Newtons first law of motion: Objects in motion tend to stay in motion.

The same happens in our mind. Our thoughts build upon each other. Positive thoughts create more positive thoughts and negative thoughts do the same. Once you begin enforcing positive habits, the snowball effect will take place. This will lead to more positive habits and more growth.

When you engage in consistent action you are creating new paradigms. These new paradigms are what separate you from the rest of the pack. These new paradigms are what will help you get ahead. Work on yourself, stay disciplined, and you will pick up speed.

"To master your mind, is to master your future." –Dabasish Mridha

ACT LIKE YOU'RE BROKE

Swallow your pride and act like you're broke. Something that helped me graduate from college debt-free was making it a habit to act like I was broke. Even when I started making good money and I had extra money to spend, I continued to tell myself otherwise. This paradigm allowed me to continue living beneath my means.

I began to attach a monetary value to everything. Physical objects, internal thoughts, verbal conversations. Everything I did was either costing me or making me money. Taking a nap cost me time—invaluable. The foul words I said to my boss cost me a raise—unfortunate. The nervous thoughts before an interview cost me a job—regretful. Throwing away leftover food cost me a few dollars—disappointing. Not washing my hands, cost me a doctor's visit—disgusting. Everything I did was costing me money either directly or indirectly.

These are things that college students don't think about. However, if you do begin to think this way, you'd be amazed with how much you'd not only begin to save, but also how much you'd begin to make.

By acting like you're broke, you'll continue to work hard, pick up more shifts, take your lunch with you everywhere you go, or buy food off the dollar menu. You will shop only when you need to, not when you want to. You'll get an apartment that is the best bang for your buck and you'll always be impeccable with your word. You will take all the hand me downs that you can get, you will buy a fuel-efficient car and most importantly, you will live frugally.

Even when you start making money, act like you're still broke. This will keep you from spending money on unnecessary things, you will get into a habit of saving, and it will become routine. This is how you will build your wealth.

"It is those who never change their minds that never change anything." – Winston S. Churchill

CHALLENGE: Take a video or write a post on what the saying "Discipline Determines Direction" means to you. Don't forget to add the hashtags #gettingahead and #ultraproductive.

MAKE YOUR DREAMS A REALITY

I know we've all daydreamed once before. A dream about a life better than the one we're currently living. For a split second it felt real, it felt attainable, it felt like you were already there.

That feeling is the law of attraction working in your favor. When you're able to visualize exactly what it is you want in life, the universe is working to make it happen. The more you visualize and the more you believe, the more you'll turn into a magnet and attract all those incredible things.

Embrace that feeling no matter how crazy it is.

For those of you who truly want to graduate college debt-free, ask, believe and you shall receive. When you believe in something strong enough, nothing can get in the way of that belief. Continue working hard, believe the universe is working in your favor and you will be amazed with how things start working for you.

You'll get that high paying job, you'll receive money from relatives, you'll attract friends who are also trying to save money, and you'll become surrounded by other students who work hard. Everything will begin to fall into your lap because you have an unwavering belief and the work ethic to back it up.

When dreams end, there is no more greatness. So, dream big, work hard, and make it happen. Start here, start now, graduate college debt-free, then go change the world. This is the beginning of a new era. Your era. This is your time to show the world what you've got. Ignore the naysayers. Do what you know is right and the rest will fall into place.

Once you change your mindset, you can attack anything. You are not responsible for all the things that happen to you, but you are completely in control of your attitude and your reactions to them.

Let your passion take the steering wheel.

Let blind faith be your compass.

Let the universe work in your favor.

"Spoke some things in the universe and they appeared." – Nipsey Hussle

FAILURE, I LOVE IT

There's a feeling that comes over a man when he receives exactly what he desires. This is a special feeling. A feeling you have the chance to experience if you follow the guidelines of this book.

The universe tends to unfold the way it should and you get what you deserve. That is why you have to fight for a great life if you want a great life. Our character is formed on the anvil of adversity. No matter the weather or the storm, we have to keep fighting.

The world can go against me, but I will still come out on top.

But in order to keep fighting, you need to first fall in love with hard work. You need to fall in love with the process. The thirty-hour weekends, the sleepless nights, the blood, sweat, and tears. You need to learn to embrace the pain and chase what makes you the most uncomfortable. Because without discomfort, there will never be growth, and there will be no getting ahead.

Call me crazy, but I loved being in the dirt. I loved being in the gutter, and being a nobody. But I never quit; I never gave up. I believed that graduating college debt-free was attainable. When it happened, I wasn't surprised because I had believed so strongly and deeply that I would graduate college debt-free that I knew nothing would stop me.

I rose like a phoenix.

Now it's your turn to be self-made. Create a better life for yourself. Fight through adversity and come out on top. By doing so on your own, you will feel a sense of pride, joy, and satisfaction like never before.

"Fortunes gravitate to men whose minds have been prepared to attract them." – Napoleon Hill

SOMEHOW, I KNEW

Starting from an early age I knew I was different. I knew, somehow, that I was destined to do something extraordinary with my life. I had a bigger vision for myself.

I didn't have to try all that hard to be different from the rest of the crowd. I naturally strayed away from the masses and focused on what felt right in my heart. My decisions came intuitively and I continued to follow the path I knew was pre-determined. Destiny was always pulling me closer.

While on this journey of bigger visions, I stayed away from the path and got caught up in superficial things: the drugs, the alcohol, the image. It led me spiraling out of control.

During my rock-bottom, I had time to reflect on my life. Time to reflect on the thoughts in my mind and the experiences I had had up until that point. I realized that I had truly let myself go.

I lied, I cheated, I stole. I didn't care about how it affected me. I didn't care about how it affected others. All the standards I had once set for myself, and the moral code I once lived by, were thrown out the window. The high expectations I once had for myself were nonexistent. I thought I had ruined my life beyond repair.

This reflection helped me see that sometimes you can't know what your best self looks like without having seen yourself at your worst. You can't feel the heights of success without the depths of failure and the weeks of depression.

This low point taught me to always set higher expectations for myself. You should too. Hold yourself to a high standard of excellence and never get content. Every day is another chance to get better.

When you feel the universe call your number, embrace that feeling and never let it go. Use it as a reminder that you have the potential to do something incredible with your life. Don't count yourself out. You can make a difference. You can make an impact. You can change the world. Conquer your thoughts and believe!

"I must first work in the dark for my light to shine." – Unknown

CHAPTER 25

DO WHAT YOU CAN BUT NOT TOO MUCH

Don't forget to treat yourself.

The point of this book is to make you work harder, not to make you unhappy. The last thing I want is for you to work yourself to overwhelm. Don't forget to appreciate all the wonderful things this world has to offer. Enjoy your friends and your family. Appreciate the sunlight, the rain, and the birds. Love others, and most importantly, don't forget to love yourself!

I like to have fun. I like to go out and enjoy myself with friends. I'm not here to advocate against that. All I'll say is the more time you spend in comfort, the less you will grow. If you're constantly doing what is fun and easy, then your life will become insignificant and hard.

However, you should also enjoy yourself from time to time. Balance is important. When things get hard and stressful, don't push yourself over the edge. It is okay to take a step back to refuel before getting back at it.

During my college days, I went through a couple rough patches. I pushed myself to the point of mental exhaustion and physical collapse. I worked more than I slept, studied more than I ate, and went to the gym more than I had the energy for.

This led me to a stint of deep depression. I stood eye to eye with darkness. My mind played cruel tricks on me and I couldn't break free no matter how hard I tried. I felt like everything around me was falling apart.

I was crying for help but too proud to reach out. I didn't talk to anyone about what was going on in my life because I didn't want my baggage to weigh anyone else down. I didn't want to be a burden. I realized that everyone had their own problems, and I didn't want mine to add to their stresses. So, I kept everything to myself.

I wanted to be the rock that held everyone together. The strong foundation that everyone could lean on. I wanted to be the well that everyone drank from. I wanted to give life to those who were closest to me. I did my best to hold everyone and everything together.

But as time went on, things got worse inside my head. I was hurting bad and it got harder and harder to see the light at the end of the tunnel. The light was fading, and my thoughts got darker.

Months of depression led me to becoming scared of myself. I couldn't escape from my thoughts. I felt trapped. I started to believe that it would be easier to just end it altogether.

I entertained this thought often.

Every day was a constant battle and a constant struggle to find happiness. I was truly hurting on the inside and couldn't see a way out. My judgment was clouded by the voices inside my head. I was near my breaking point.

By the grace of God, I found salvation despite the darkness all around me. My thoughts haunted me, but they were no match for the Lord.

This period in my life taught me that there is more to life than making money and getting ahead. If you're going through something difficult, make sure to talk to someone.

There is no shame in talking to someone about your problems—your pain, anxiety, and hopelessness. Your mind and body can only handle so much. You can only handle so many missed meals, sleepless nights, and hours at work. You can only push yourself so hard before you breakdown from mental and emotional strain.

We all need help.

If you're in a dark place, I promise it will get better. The sun always rises after the darkness of the night. Just keep moving forward. One day you'll look back on everything you went through and understand why. Right now, you just have to trust that brighter days are waiting ahead.

HEALTH TIPS FOR YOU

When life gets difficult, use these five tips to naturally boost endorphins and refresh your mind!

- **Drink Green Tea** – It turns out green tea can make you happier. In a study published by Public Health Nutrition, people who drank about four cups of green tea per day were half as likely to feel depressed than people who didn't drink green tea.

154

- **Lemon Juice** – Lemon juice provides your body with energy when it enters your digestive tract, and it also helps reduce anxiety and depression. (Even the *scent* of lemons has a calming effect on your nervous system!)

- **Sunlight** – Sunlight has more than one health benefit to offer. It helps your skin produce vitamin D, an essential nutrient. It also boosts production of serotonin and melatonin which can help improve your mood, increase your energy, and help you get better sleep.

- **Cold Showers** – Cold showers can work as a kind of gentle electroshock therapy. The cold water sends many electrical impulses to your brain. They jolt your system to increase alertness, clarity, and energy levels.

- **Dark Chocolate** – Consuming dark chocolate will help improve your mood and make you feel calmer and more content, partly because dark chocolate stimulates the production of endorphins, the chemicals in the brain that create feelings of pleasure.

CHAPTER 26

...AND THEN WRITE A BOOK ABOUT IT

The best part about accomplishing something big is being able to share the journey. Your story should be heard if it can help other people. If you have something that is good, you have an obligation to offer it to the world. Don't be afraid to create a new path. Sooner or later others will follow.

In the short time that I was at Austin Community College and Texas State, all I wanted to do was leave an impact. I tried to get other people to look at life differently. I wanted to try and do things different from the masses. Something incredible and uncommon. Then I wanted to share my story so others could be inspired to share stories of their own.

Looking back, the journey to graduating college debt-free was worth it. Sometimes I sit outside, watch the sunset, and think about how far I've come. The jobs I've worked, the people I've met, the sacrifices I've made, and I can't help but smile—because I know after reading this book, someone out there will graduate college debt-free too.

I'll leave you on this note:

Stay true to yourself and never give up. You can make a difference, you can make an impact, and you can change the world. You are here to break the generational curse. You are here to touch the lives of many. Have faith in your abilities and you'll accomplish amazing things. Believe in yourself and don't forget to enjoy the journey. Now go build your empire!

"The ones who are crazy enough to think that they can change the world, are the ones that do." – Steve Jobs

TEN BOOKS THAT CHANGED MY LIFE

1) Think & Grow Rich by Napoleon Hill

2) The Compound Effect by Darren Hardy

3) The Secret by Rhonda Byrne

4) Life's Instructions for Wisdom, Success, and Happiness by H. Jackson Brown Jr.

5) The Slight Edge by Jeff Olson

6) The Subtle Art of Not Giving A Fuck by Mark Mason

7) The Richest Man in Babylon by George S. Clason

8) Rhinoceros Success by Scott Alexander

9) The Power of Now by Eckhart Tolle

10) Wooden: A Lifetime of Observations and Reflections On and Off the Court by John Wooden

NOTES

https://www.huffingtonpost.ca/2015/01/15/green-tea-benefits_n_6477258.html

https://recipegeek.com/food-talk/health-wellness/8-reasons-you-should-be-drinking-lemon-water-every-morning

https://www.healthline.com/health/depression/benefits-sunlight

https://www.healthline.com/health/cold-shower-benefits

https://www.inc.com/jeff-haden/scientists-just-discovered-that-eating-chocolate-has-an-amazing-affect-on-happiness-but-there-is-a-literally-small-catch.html

ABOUT
KHARIS PUBLISHING

KHARIS PUBLISHING is an independent, traditional publishing house with a core mission to publish impactful books, and channel proceeds into establishing mini-libraries or resource centers for orphanages in developing countries, so these kids will learn to read, dream, and grow. Every time you purchase a book from Kharis Publishing or partner as an author, you are helping give these kids an amazing opportunity to read, dream, and grow. Kharis Publishing is an imprint of Kharis Media LLC. Learn more at
https://www.kharispublishing.com.

CPSIA information can be obtained
at www.ICGtesting.com
Printed in the USA
FSHW022147310121
78202FS